Easy
DOES IT

CREATIVE DECOR AND SO MUCH MORE!

*M*ore and more today, we seem to have less and less time
for the things that brighten our lives — shopping, decorating,
and choosing gifts for the ones we love. To help you make the
most of your precious time, we've combined the quickest and
easiest clothing, decorating, and gift projects we've ever developed
into one fantastic volume — Easy Does It! You'll find that
dressing up your decor is fast and simple with our no-hassle,
no-mistake methods. Use our time-saving ideas to create accents
like fabulous table toppers, cozy pillows, and even decorator-look
window treatments! And when you need a special gift, turn to
our delightful collection of tokens to express your affection.
We've also designed a closetful of fun and affordable fashions
— and most are crafted without sewing a single stitch.
Starting today, when you want something special, make
it easy and then take it easy with Easy Does It!

Anne Childs

LEISURE ARTS, INC.
Little Rock, Arkansas

Easy DOES IT

CREATIVE DECOR AND SO MUCH MORE!

EDITORIAL STAFF

Editor-in-Chief: Anne Van Wagner Childs
Executive Director: Sandra Graham Case
Executive Editor: Susan Frantz Wiles
Publications Director: Carla Bentley
Creative Art Director: Gloria Bearden
Production Art Director: Melinda Stout

DESIGN
Design Director: Patricia Wallenfang Sowers
Designers: Janice M. Adams, Diana Heien Suttle, Linda Diehl Tiano, Rebecca Sunwall Werle, and Donna Waldrip Pittard
Design Assistant: Kathy Jones

TECHNICAL
Managing Editor: Kathy Rose Bradley
Senior Editor: Leslie Schick Gorrell
Technical Writers: Chanda English Adams, Emily Jane Barefoot, Candice Treat Murphy, Kimberly J. Smith, and Ann Brawner Turner

EDITORIAL
Associate Editor: Linda L. Trimble
Senior Editorial Writer: Tammi Williamson Bradley
Editorial Writers: Terri Leming Davidson, Jonathon Walker, Amy Manning-Nelson, Marla Shivers, and Sonya Young
Copy Editor: Laura Lee Weland

ART
Book/Magazine Art Director: Diane M. Ghegan
Senior Production Artist: Michael A. Spigner
Photography Stylists: Christina Tiano, Charlisa Erwin Parker, Sondra Daniel, Wanda Young, Karen Smart Hall, and Laura Bushmiaer

ADVERTISING AND DIRECT MAIL
Senior Editor: Tena Kelley Vaughn
Copywriter: Steven M. Cooper
Designer: Rhonda H. Hestir
Art Director: Jeff Curtis
Production Artists: Linda Lovette Smart and Angie Griffin
Typesetters: Cindy Lumpkin and Larry Flaxman

BUSINESS STAFF

Publisher: Steve Patterson
Controller: Tom Siebenmorgen
Retail Sales Director: Richard Tignor
Retail Marketing Director: Pam Stebbins
Retail Customer Services Director: Margaret Sweetin
Marketing Manager: Russ Barnett

Executive Director of Marketing and Circulation: Guy A. Crossley
Fulfillment Manager: Byron L. Taylor
Print Production Manager: Laura Lockhart
Print Production Coordinator: Nancy Reddick Lister

Table of Contents

EASY DOES IT DECORATING 6

Table of Contents

EASY DOES IT GIFTS 62

Table of Contents

EASY DOES IT FASHIONS 90

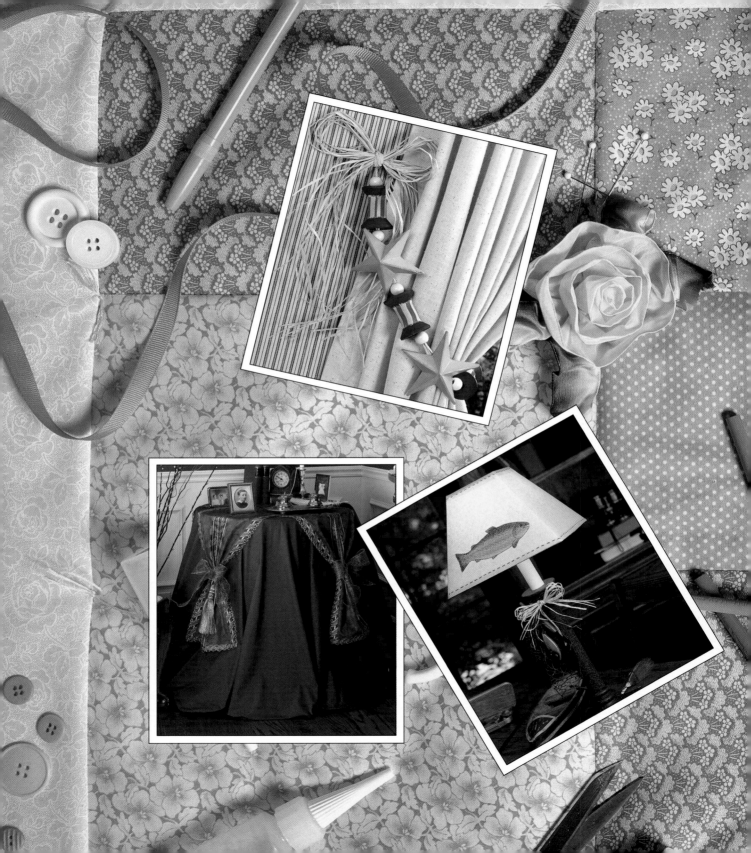

Easy
DOES IT
DECORATING

*S*ometimes redecorating a room simply means re-doing the accents. Cozy pillows tossed in a favorite old chair, lamps topped with bright new shades, and even decorative tiebacks for the curtains can awaken your decor with life and color. With these clever projects and many more, we'll show you easy — and inexpensive — ways to cheer up your kitchen, brighten the bedroom, or revive any room you choose. Just mix our project ideas with fabrics to match your home interior, and before you know it, your house will have a great new look!

FAST AND FABULOUS

Dressing up your decor is fast and simple when you use our wonderful no-sew techniques to create fabulous fabric covers. Set a rich tone by selecting opulent prints and then glue on distinctive trims to create the skirted toppers. Whether draping an inexpensive accent table or a timeworn ottoman, these pleasing pieces are an elegant, easy way to perk up a corner.

Crisscross Table Runners, page 11
Pouf Table Skirt, page 10

Gilded details help transform a plain decorator table into a splendid display. Simply arrange the skirt (it's really a bed sheet!) into elegant poufs and top it with crisscrossed table runners in a stately print.

Bring new life to a worn ottoman in no time by creating a custom-made cover. We added extra padding to the top, covered it with durable fabric, and glued on a matching band and cording.

Custom-Covered Ottoman, page 11

A tasseled edging provides a charming finish to this round table topper. It covers an artfully poufed skirt, which we created using a richly colored bed sheet.

Fringed Round Table Topper, page 10
Pouf Table Skirt, page 10

POUF TABLE SKIRT

(Shown on pages 8 and 9)

Note: Please familiarize yourself with *Using Fusible Products*, pages 125 - 127, before beginning this project.

You will need either fabric for skirt and 1"w paper-backed fusible web tape or a flat sheet large enough to cover table and extend to floor with approx. 20" extra on each side for poufs, and tissue paper (optional).

1. (*Note:* If using a sheet, follow Step 3.) Follow *Measuring Tables,* this page, to measure table for floor length table skirt; add 42". Cut a square of fabric the determined measurement, piecing with web tape if necessary.
2. Follow *Making a Single Hem*, page 127, to make a 1" hem along edges of skirt.
3. Center skirt or sheet on table. Tuck edges under at floor and arrange folds for "pouf" effect. If desired, stuff poufs with tissue paper to maintain shape.

FRINGED ROUND TABLE TOPPER (Shown on page 9)

Note: Please familiarize yourself with *Using Fusible Products*, pages 125 - 127, before beginning this project.

You will need fabric for topper, 1"w paper-backed fusible web tape, 2" long tassel fringe, liquid fray preventative, fabric glue, string, fabric marking pencil, and thumbtack or pin.

1. Follow *Measuring Tables*, this page, to measure table for desired drop length of table topper (not including fringe); add 2".
2. Cut a fabric square the measurement determined in Step 1, piecing with web tape if necessary.
3. To mark cutting line, fold fabric square in half from top to bottom and again from left to right. Tie 1 end of string to fabric marking pencil. Measure 1/2 the measurement determined in Step 1 from pencil. Insert thumbtack through string at this point. Insert thumbtack through fabric as shown in Fig. 1 and mark 1/4 of a circle. Cut along drawn line through all fabric layers.

Fig. 1

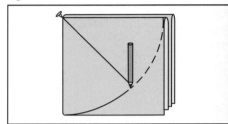

4. Follow *Making a Single Hem*, page 127, to make a 1" hem along edge of fabric circle.
5. With tassels extending beyond edge of table topper, glue straight edge of tassel fringe along edge on right side of table topper, trimming to fit. Apply fray preventative to ends of fringe. Allow to dry flat.
6. Center table topper on table.

MEASURING TABLES

Note: When measuring tables, always use a metal measuring tape; fabric tapes can sag or stretch.

Refer to Diagram to measure round tables for table skirts or table toppers, measuring across tabletop at widest point and to desired length on each side. Refer to project instructions for amount to add to measurement for hems or edge treatment.

DIAGRAM

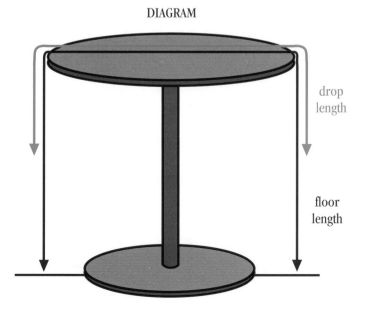

drop length

floor length

CRISSCROSS TABLE RUNNERS
(Shown on page 8)

Note: Please familiarize yourself with *Using Fusible Products*, pages 125 - 127, before beginning this project.

For each table runner, you will need fabric for table runner, 1"w paper-backed fusible web tape, 1" long gold loop fringe, 1½"w flat gold trim, 3"w gold mesh ribbon for bows, two large gold tassels, 2 small gold safety pins, liquid fray preventative, and fabric glue.

1. (*Note:* Follow Steps 1 - 5 to make each table runner.) To determine size of fabric piece, determine desired finished width of table runner; add 4". Follow *Measuring Tables,* page 10, to measure table for desired drop length of table runner; add 4". Cut a piece of fabric the determined measurements.

2. Follow *Making a Double Hem*, page 127, to make a 1" hem along each side edge and each end of table runner.

3. With right side of fringe facing wrong side of table runner, glue loop fringe along each side edge of table runner with fringe extending approx. ½" beyond edges of table runner; trim to fit. Apply fray preventative to ends of fringe. Allow to dry flat.

4. Glue flat trim along each end on right side of table runner, trimming to fit. Apply fray preventative to ends of trim. Allow to dry flat.

5. Tie gold mesh ribbon into a bow around each end of table runner; trim ribbon ends. Use safety pin on wrong side of runner to attach 1 tassel behind knot of each bow.

6. With table runners crossing at center of tabletop, center runners on table.

CUSTOM-COVERED OTTOMAN (Shown on page 9)

Note: Please familiarize yourself with *Using Fusible Products*, pages 125 - 127, before beginning this project.

You will need a round ottoman (we found ours at a local thrift shop), medium to heavyweight fabric to cover ottoman, 2" thick foam rubber as large as top of ottoman, electric knife, 1"w paper-backed fusible web tape, border-print fabric for trim (our trim fabric strip measured 4¾"w before hemming), ½" dia. cording with flange, brown craft paper or newspaper, string, removable fabric marking pen, T-pins, thumbtack or pin, fabric glue, hot glue gun, and glue sticks.

1. For foam rubber pad pattern, place ottoman top side down on craft paper. Use a pencil to draw around top of ottoman; cut out pattern.

2. Use fabric marking pen to draw around pattern on foam rubber. Keeping blade of knife straight up-and-down, use electric knife to cut circle from foam rubber.

3. Place foam rubber circle on top of ottoman; hot glue in place. Refer to Fig. 1 to measure from bottom of 1 side of ottoman to bottom of opposite side; add 4".

Fig. 1

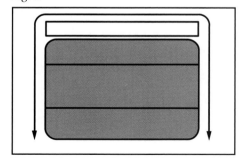

4. Cut a square of fabric the determined measurement, piecing with web tape if necessary.

5. To mark cutting line, fold fabric square in half from top to bottom and again from left to right. Tie 1 end of string to fabric marking pen. Measure ½ the measurement determined in Step 3 from pen. Insert thumbtack through string at this point. Insert thumbtack through fabric as shown in Fig. 1 of Fringed Round Table Topper instructions, page 10, and mark ¼ of a circle. Cut along drawn line through all fabric layers.

6. Follow *Making a Single Hem*, page 127, to make a 1" hem along edge of fabric circle.

7. (*Note:* To prevent ends of cording from fraying after cutting, apply fabric glue to ½" of cording around area to be cut, allow to dry, and then cut.) Hot glue flange of cording along hemmed edge on wrong side of fabric circle; trimming to fit.

8. Place cover over ottoman. Working from 1 side then the other, pull fabric taut across top of ottoman, securing fabric with T-pins below foam rubber.

9. For trim, measure around top of ottoman; add 2". Determine desired finished width of trim; add 2". Cut a strip of fabric the determined measurements.

10. Follow *Making a Single Hem*, page 127, to make a 1" hem along 1 end and along long edges of trim fabric strip. Beginning with unhemmed end, wrap trim tightly around ottoman with 1 long edge just below top edge of ottoman. Hot glue trim in place. Remove T-pins if desired.

TERRIFIC TIEBACKS

*Give your curtains a brand-new look with these creative tiebacks! They're
all easy to craft using simple, inexpensive supplies. From a fringed fabric napkin
to a garland of dried fruits, these clever drapery decorations will enhance
any decor with ease and style — and let your personality shine.*

Kitchen Napkin Tiebacks, page 15

*A checked picnic napkin will add a dash of down-home charm to your kitchen or breakfast nook. For another bright look,
try the silk sunflower tiebacks shown on our front cover.*

(Left) *Featuring fabric scraps and an assortment of sewing notions, this tieback is perfect for your hobby room. The "stitches" are drawn with a felt-tip pen.*

(Below, left) *Dried fruits, nuts, cinnamon sticks, and cookie cutters are added to a purchased berry garland to create our unique tieback. Inexpensive and easy to make, it'll spice up any room!*

(Below, right) *Transform plain into patriotic with an all-American tieback! Simply string wooden beads and fabric-accented spools on strands of raffia, then glue on papier-mâché stars and finish with a big bow.*

Sewing Enthusiast's Tiebacks, page 14

Fruit Garland Tiebacks, page 14

Stars and Spools Tiebacks, page 15

FRUIT GARLAND TIEBACKS (Shown on page 13)

For each pair of tiebacks, you will need wired berry garland, purchased dried orange and apple slices (available at craft stores and florist shops), whole cinnamon sticks, assorted nuts, metal cookie cutters, one $1/4$" x 9" torn fabric strip for hanger for each cookie cutter, wire cutters, 2 cup hooks, hot glue gun, and glue sticks.

1. To determine length of each tieback, measure around curtain by holding a tape measure loosely at desired position of tieback; add 2". Cut two lengths of garland the determined measurement.

2. (*Note:* Follow remaining steps for each tieback.) Fold 1 garland length in half and mark center point with a pencil. Unfold garland and lay flat on work surface. Beginning at center mark and working to 1" from 1 end of garland, glue orange and apple slices, cinnamon sticks, and nuts to garland as desired; for each cookie cutter, thread 1 torn fabric strip through cookie cutter and knot strip around garland (decorate opposite end of second tieback).

3. Screw a cup hook into window trim or wall next to curtain at desired height of tieback. Wrap garland around curtain and twist ends together. Hang twisted garland ends on cup hook.

SEWING ENTHUSIAST'S TIEBACKS (Shown on page 13)

Note: Please familiarize yourself with *Using Fusible Products, General Information,* page 125, before beginning this project.

For each pair of tiebacks, you will need fabric for tiebacks, two 7" torn squares of muslin, two 7" torn squares of print fabric, two $3/4$" x 11" torn fabric strips for bows, scrap fabric for heart appliqués, two 7" squares of polyester bonded batting, thread to match tieback fabric, paper-backed fusible web, two $41/2$" dia. wooden embroidery hoops, items to decorate tiebacks (we used a needle threaded with floss, buttons, a safety pin, and miniature wooden spools of thread), 2 small and 2 large safety pins, 2 cup hooks, black felt-tip pen with fine point, tracing paper, hot glue gun, and glue sticks.

1. To determine length of each tieback, measure around curtain by holding a tape measure loosely at desired position of tieback; add 12$1/2$". Cut one 10"w fabric strip the determined measurement for each tieback.

2. Trace lettering pattern onto tracing paper; set aside.

3. (*Note:* Follow remaining steps for each tieback.) Matching right sides and long edges, fold one 10"w fabric strip in half; press. Leaving an opening for turning, use a $1/4$" seam allowance to sew raw edges together. Clip corners, turn right side out, and press; hand stitch opening closed.

4. To transfer lettering pattern to 1 muslin square, use a pencil to draw over grey lines of pattern on back of tracing paper. Center pattern right side up on muslin square. Use the edge of a penny or spoon to rub over pattern. Remove pattern.

5. For heart appliqué, trace heart pattern onto paper side of web. Cutting approx. $1/2$" outside drawn lines, cut out heart. Follow manufacturer's instructions to fuse heart to wrong side of appliqué fabric. Cut out heart along drawn lines.

6. Remove paper backing from heart. Position heart on muslin and fuse in place.

7. Use black pen to draw over transferred lines on muslin and to draw dashed lines just inside edges of heart to resemble stitching.

8. Place muslin right side up on 1 batting square; center muslin and batting in hoop. Trim excess batting close to hoop.

9. Arrange hoop with muslin square at an angle over 1 print fabric square; glue to secure.

10. Attach or glue decorative items to edges of muslin as desired.

11. Tie 1 torn fabric strip into a bow. Glue bow to top of hoop.

12. Screw a cup hook into window trim or wall next to curtain at desired height of tieback. Wrap tieback around curtain and place ends together. Pinch tieback 6" from ends to gather; place a large safety pin around tieback to hold gathers. Use a small safety pin to pin hoop to tieback over gathers. Hang large safety pin on cup hook.

KITCHEN NAPKIN TIEBACKS

(Shown on page 12)

Note: Please familiarize yourself with *Using Fusible Products*, *General Information*, page 125, before beginning this project.

For each pair of tiebacks, you will need a large fringed reversible square napkin (we used a 17" square woven cotton napkin), $1/2$"w paper-backed fusible web tape, coordinating embroidery floss, two 1" dia. buttons, 2 small cabone rings (plastic curtain rings), and 2 cup hooks.

1. Fold napkin in half diagonally; press. Unfold napkin and cut in half along fold.
2. (*Note:* Follow remaining steps for each tieback.) Follow *Making a Single Hem*, page 127, to make a $1/2$" hem along raw edge of napkin. Press hemmed edge $1 1/2$" to 1 side (right side). Using 6 strands of floss and *Running Stitch*, page 124, stitch $1/4$" from hemmed edge (Fig. 1).

Fig. 1

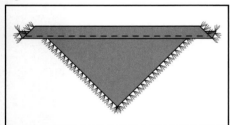

3. With right side facing out and matching top edges, fold tieback in half. Stitching through all layers of fabric, use floss to sew 1 button to front of tieback at top outside corner (sew button to opposite side of second tieback). Sew cabone ring to back of tieback behind button.
4. Screw a cup hook into window trim or wall next to curtain at desired height of tieback. Slip tieback over curtain and hang cabone ring on cup hook.

STARS AND SPOOLS TIEBACKS (Shown on page 13)

For each pair of tiebacks, you will need natural raffia, 4" dia. papier-mâché stars (we used 2 stars for each of our 14" wide tiebacks), 2" long wooden spools (we used 3 for each tieback), fabric to cover spools, $5/8$" dia. white wooden beads (we used 6 for each tieback), dark yellow and dark blue acrylic spray paint, Design Master® glossy wood tone spray (available at craft stores and florist shops), 2 cup hooks, craft glue, hot glue gun, and glue sticks.

1. Spray paint stars dark yellow and spools dark blue. Allow to dry. Lightly spray stars with wood tone spray. Allow to dry.
2. Measure length of center of 1 spool; measure around center of spool and add $1/4$". Tear a strip of fabric the determined measurements for each spool. Overlapping ends, use craft glue to glue 1 fabric strip around each spool.
3. Knot 5 strands of raffia together at center. To determine length of each tieback, loosely knot raffia strands around curtain at desired position of tieback with center knot at inside edge of curtain; trim ends to desired length. Use a pencil to lightly mark location of second knot on raffia (Fig. 1). Untie second knot in raffia and remove from curtain.

Fig. 1

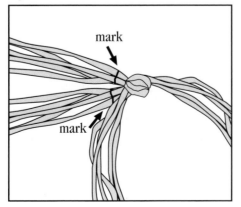

4. For second tieback, use knotted strands of raffia as a guide and knot 5 more strands of raffia together at center, trim ends to length, and mark placement of second knot on strands.
5. (*Note:* Follow remaining steps for each tieback.) Positioning items next to center knot, thread 1 bead, 1 spool, and another bead onto 1 end of 1 raffia length. Hot glue 1 star next to last bead. Continue threading beads and spools and gluing stars onto 1 end of raffia until items extend to pencil mark on raffia (decorate opposite end of second tieback).
6. Screw a cup hook into window trim or wall next to curtain at desired height of tieback. Matching pencil marks on raffia, knot tieback around curtain and hang knot of tieback on cup hook.
7. Tie several strands of raffia into a bow; trim ends. Secure back of bow on cup hook over knot of tieback.

SUNFLOWER TIEBACKS

(Shown on cover)

Each of our sunny floral tiebacks is simply crafted from a 24" long purchased braided raffia dangle (available at craft stores) and 6" dia. silk sunflowers.

For each tieback, fold braided raffia dangle in half and mark center point lightly with a pencil. Remove several silk sunflowers and leaves from stems. Hot glue flowers and leaves as desired to braided raffia dangle between center mark and knot at 1 end (decorate opposite end of second tieback).

Screw a cup hook into window trim or wall next to curtain at desired height of tieback. Wrap tieback around curtain and hang ends on cup hook.

PILLOW TALK

*Nothing adds a sense of comfort and style to a room as quickly as a few accent pillows.
Whether you prefer a look that's nostalgic or contemporary, you'll love our four cushy
collections, all created using three basic shapes and super-easy no-sew techniques.
In no time, these splendid notions will be ready to brighten your home!*

Envelope Pillow with Corsage, page 21
Fringed Parlor Pillow, page 20

*The Victorian envelope pillow features a pinned-on silk corsage and elegant fringe held in place with fabric glue.
The square fringed pillow is created with lush coordinating fabrics and trims. (Opposite) Richly patterned fabrics in
neutral shades complement a traditional decor. One pillow has a fused-on patchwork design, and a tassel dresses
up the envelope pillow. The ends of the roll pillow are secured with rubber bands.*

Elegant Envelope Pillow, page 21
Banded Roll Pillow, page 20
Traditional Square Pillow, page 21

Sprucing up his favorite room will be a cinch with these handsome pillows (below). The dapper necktie design is fused together using timeworn menswear, and the argyle pillow sports a dynamic combination of fabrics and dimensional paint. (Opposite) Our country cushions can be made in a flash for a simple homespun look. The whimsical birdhouse and garden fence pillows combine transferred designs shaded with colored pencils and fused appliqués cut from plaids and ginghams. A decorated wooden heart lends a warm touch to the envelope pillow.

Argyle Pillow, page 23
Tie Pillow, page 23

Feathered-Friend Pillow, page 22
Country Envelope Pillow, page 22
Country Garden Pillow, page 22

FRINGED PARLOR PILLOW (Shown on page 16)

Note: Please familiarize yourself with *Using Fusible Products*, pages 125 - 127, before beginning this project.

For a 15" square pillow, you will need two 15¹/₂" fabric squares for pillow, one 10" fabric square for panel on front of pillow, 1¹/₄ yds of 1¹/₂"w loop fringe, 2³/₄ yds of ¹/₂"w gimp trim, 2 yds of ¹/₂" dia. cording with ¹/₂" flange, paper-backed fusible web, ³/₄"w paper-backed fusible web tape, polyester fiberfill, spring-type clothespins, fabric glue, and liquid fray preventative.

1. Follow manufacturer's instructions to fuse web to wrong side of 10" fabric square. Remove paper backing. Center and fuse square to right side of one 15¹/₂" fabric square (pillow front).

2. Glue loop fringe along edges of 10" fabric square, mitering fringe at corners and trimming ends to fit. Glue gimp trim along inner edge of fringe. Apply fray preventative to ends of trims. Allow to dry flat.

3. (*Note:* To prevent ends of cording from fraying after cutting, apply fabric glue to ¹/₂" of cording around area to be cut, allow to dry, and then cut.) For pillow, fuse web tape along edges on right side of pillow front. Remove paper backing. Beginning 2" from 1 end of cording, fuse flange of cording to pillow front, clipping flange at corners (Fig. 1); trim ends of cording to 1" from pillow front.

Fig. 1

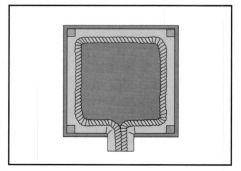

4. Fuse web tape to flange of cording along edge of pillow front except where free ends of cording meet. Remove paper backing.

5. Place pillow pieces right sides together. Leaving a 6" area open for turning and stuffing where ends of cording meet, fuse edges of pillow pieces together. Do not clip seam allowances at corners. Turn pillow right side out and carefully push corners outward, making sure seam allowances lie flat. Being careful not to fuse opening, press pillow.

6. Stuff pillow with fiberfill. Cross ends of cording and tuck ends inside pillow (Fig. 2). Fuse edges of pillow together at opening. Where cording crosses, glue fabric and cording together as necessary; secure with clothespins until glue is dry.

Fig. 2

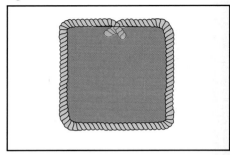

7. Glue gimp trim to pillow front along inner edge of cording, trimming ends to fit. Apply fray preventative to ends of trim. Use clothespins to secure trim until glue is dry.

BANDED ROLL PILLOW (Shown on page 17)

Note: Please familiarize yourself with *Using Fusible Products*, pages 125 - 127, before beginning this project.

For an approx. 6" dia. x 25" long pillow, you will need a 21" x 35" fabric piece for pillow, a 6" x 21" fabric piece for band, paper-backed fusible web, 1"w paper-backed fusible web tape, two 21" lengths of ⁵/₈"w decorative flat trim, two 7" lengths of ³/₈" dia. twisted satin cord, 2 rubber bands, polyester fiberfill, spring-type clothespins, and fabric glue.

1. To hem each short edge of pillow fabric piece, follow manufacturer's instructions to fuse web tape along short edge on wrong side of pillow fabric piece. Do not remove paper backing. Press edge 5" to wrong side. Unfold edge and remove paper backing. Refold edge and fuse in place.

2. Follow manufacturer's instructions to fuse web to wrong side of band fabric piece. Remove paper backing. Matching ends of band with raw edges of pillow fabric piece, center and fuse band to right side of pillow fabric piece.

3. Center and glue trim over raw edges of band. Allow to dry flat.

4. Fuse web tape along raw edges on right side of pillow fabric piece. Remove paper backing. Matching right sides and raw edges, fold fabric piece in half. Fuse raw edges together to form a tube. Press seam allowance to 1 side. Turn tube right side out.

5. Wrap 1 rubber band around 1 end of tube 3" from end. Stuff tube firmly with fiberfill to 3" from remaining end. Wrap remaining rubber band around tube 3" from end.

6. (*Note:* To prevent ends of cord from fraying after cutting, apply fabric glue to ¹/₂" of cord around area to be cut, allow to dry, and then cut.) Wrap 1 cord length around each rubber band, trimming to fit. Glue ends of cord together to secure; secure with clothespins until glue is dry.

ENVELOPE PILLOW WITH CORSAGE (Shown on page 16)

Note: Please familiarize yourself with *Using Fusible Products*, pages 125 - 127, before beginning this project.

For an 18½" x 13" pillow, you will need a 15" x 20½" fabric piece for pillow front, a 20½" x 23¼"fabric piece for pillow back and flap, ⅞ yd of 1⅞"w loop fringe, ⅞ yd of ½"w gimp trim, 1"w paper-backed fusible web tape, polyester fiberfill, silk flowers with leaves, 1½"w and 3"w assorted ribbons, florist wire, wire cutters, large safety pin, 1½" of ¾"w hook and loop fastener tape, spring-type clothespins, liquid fray preventative, fabric glue, hot glue gun, and glue sticks.

1. For flap on pillow back fabric piece, fuse web tape along 1 short edge (top edge) of pillow back fabric piece. Do not remove paper backing. Fold top corners diagonally to wrong side and press (Fig. 1). Unfold corners and remove paper backing. Refold corners and fuse in place.

Fig. 1

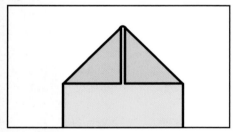

2. Follow *Making a Single Hem*, page 127, to make a 1" hem along 1 long edge (top edge) of pillow front fabric piece.
3. Fuse web tape along remaining edges on right side of pillow front fabric piece. Remove paper backing. Matching side and bottom edges, place pillow front and pillow back fabric pieces right sides together. Fuse edges together. Do not clip seam allowances at corners. Turn pillow right side out and carefully push corners outward, making sure seam allowances lie flat. Press pillow.

4. (*Note:* Refer to photo and use fabric glue for Step 4. Use clothespins to secure trims until glue is dry.) For trim on flap, fold 1 end of loop fringe ½" to wrong side; glue to secure. Beginning with folded end at 1 side of flap, glue loop fringe along edges of flap, mitering fringe at point; fold remaining end ½" to wrong side at opposite side of flap, trimming to fit, and glue in place. Repeat to glue gimp trim along top edge of fringe.

5. For corsage, wire flowers together. Tie ribbons into a bow; trim ends. Apply fray preventative to ribbon ends; allow to dry. Wire bow to flowers. Use safety pin on wrong side of flap to pin corsage to flap.
6. Making sure tape lengths will meet, hot glue 1 side of hook and loop fastener tape to inside of flap and 1 side to front of pillow. Stuff pillow with fiberfill. Close hook and loop fastener.

ELEGANT ENVELOPE PILLOW (Shown on page 17)

Note: Please familiarize yourself with *Using Fusible Products*, pages 125 - 127, before beginning this project.

For an 18½" x 13" envelope pillow, you will need a 15" x 20½" fabric piece for pillow front, a 20½" x 23¼" fabric piece for pillow back and flap, ⅞ yd of ⅝"w decorative flat trim, 4½" long decorative tassel, 1"w paper-backed fusible web tape, polyester fiberfill, 1½" of ¾"w hook and loop fastener tape, spring-type clothespins, fabric glue, hot glue gun, and glue sticks.

1. To make pillow, follow Steps 1 - 3 of Envelope Pillow with Corsage instructions, this page.

2. (*Note:* Refer to photo and use fabric glue for Step 2. Use clothespins to secure trim until glue is dry.) For trim on flap, fold 1 end of trim ½" to wrong side; glue to secure. Beginning with folded end at 1 side of flap, glue trim along edges of flap, mitering fringe at point; fold remaining end ½" to wrong side at opposite side of flap, trimming to fit, and glue in place.
3. Hot glue hanging loop of tassel to wrong side of flap at point.
4. To complete pillow, follow Step 6 of Envelope Pillow with Corsage instructions, this page.

TRADITIONAL SQUARE PILLOW (Shown on page 17)

Note: Please familiarize yourself with *Using Fusible Products*, pages 125 - 127, before beginning this project.

For a 15" square pillow, you will need a 15" square pillow form, two 16½" fabric squares for pillow front and back, one 8" and four 4¼" squares of contrasting fabric for pillow front, four 15" lengths of ⅝"w trims (we used 2 kinds), paper-backed fusible web, ¾"w paper-backed fusible web tape, fabric glue, and liquid fray preventative.

1. Follow manufacturer's instructions to fuse web to wrong sides of 8" and 4¼" fabric squares; remove paper backing. Referring to photo, arrange squares on one 16½" fabric square (pillow front); fuse in place.
2. For pillow, follow *Making a Basic Pillow*, page 127.
3. Center and glue trims along raw edges of fabric squares on pillow front, overlapping trims as desired. Apply fray preventative to ends of trims. Allow to dry.

FEATHERED-FRIEND PILLOW
(Shown on page 19)

Note: Please familiarize yourself with *Using Fusible Products*, pages 125 - 127, before beginning this project.

For a 12" x 17" pillow, you will need a 9" x 14" fabric piece for pillow front, fabrics for birdhouse appliqué, two 3" x 9" and two 3" x 18" fabric strips for borders, a 13" x 18" fabric piece for pillow back, paper-backed fusible web, 1/2"w paper-backed fusible web tape, polyester fiberfill, colored pencils, matte clear acrylic spray, tracing paper, graphite transfer paper, and a black felt-tip pen with fine point.

1. For birdhouse appliqués, leave at least 1" between patterns and trace birdhouse, birdhouse roof, and hole patterns, page 23, onto paper side of web. Draw a 1/2" x 6" rectangle on web for pole. Cutting approx. 1/2" outside drawn lines, cut out shapes. Follow manufacturer's instructions to fuse shapes to wrong sides of appliqué fabrics. Cut out shapes along drawn lines.
2. (*Note:* Refer to photo for remaining steps.) Remove paper backing from appliqués. Matching 1 end of pole appliqué with bottom edge of pillow front fabric piece, arrange birdhouse appliqués on pillow front fabric piece, overlapping as necessary. Fuse in place.
3. For borders, follow Step 3 of Country Garden Pillow instructions, this page.
4. For bird and flowers, trace bird and flower patterns onto tracing paper. Use transfer paper to transfer designs onto pillow front.
5. Use black pen to draw over transferred lines. Use colored pencils to color designs as desired. Lightly spray designs with acrylic spray to set designs; allow to dry.
6. For pillow, follow *Making a Basic Pillow*, page 127.

COUNTRY ENVELOPE PILLOW
(Shown on page 19)

Note: Please familiarize yourself with *Using Fusible Products*, pages 125 - 127, before beginning this project.

For an 18 1/2" x 13" pillow, you will need a 15" x 20 1/2" fabric piece for pillow front; a 20 1/2" x 23 1/4" fabric piece for pillow back and flap; two 2 1/8" x 14" fabric strips for binding; two 1" x 13" torn fabric strips for trim; 1/2"w and 1"w paper-backed fusible web tape; polyester fiberfill; 4" long unfinished wooden heart cutout; colored pencils; tracing paper; graphite transfer paper; black felt-tip pen with fine point; 1 1/2" of 3/4"w hook and loop fastener tape; matte clear acrylic spray; hot glue gun; and glue sticks.

1. To make pillow, use 1"w web tape and follow Steps 1 - 3 of Envelope Pillow with Corsage instructions, page 21.
2. For binding on flap, follow *Making a Single Hem*, page 127, to make a 1/2" hem along each end of binding strips. Use 1/2"w web tape and follow *Making Binding*, page 127, to make binding from strips.
3. Insert 1 edge of flap into fold of 1 binding strip; fuse in place. Repeat to fuse remaining binding strip to remaining edge of flap.
4. Center and fuse 1"w web tape to wrong side of each torn fabric strip. Remove paper backing. With ends of strips overlapping at point, place strips on flap, covering top edges of binding; fuse in place.
5. For heart, trace desired flower pattern onto tracing paper. Use transfer paper to transfer flower onto heart. Use black pen to draw over transferred lines. Use colored pencils to color flower as desired. Lightly spray heart with acrylic spray; allow to dry. Hot glue heart to flap.
6. To complete pillow, follow Step 6 of Envelope Pillow with Corsage instructions, page 21.

COUNTRY GARDEN PILLOW
(Shown on page 19)

Note: Please familiarize yourself with *Using Fusible Products*, pages 125 - 127, before beginning this project.

For a 12" square pillow, you will need a 9" fabric square for pillow front, an 8" fabric square for fence appliqué, two 2 1/2" x 9" and two 2 1/2" x 12" fabric strips for borders, a 12" fabric square for pillow back, two 2 1/8" x 12" and two 2 1/8" x 13" fabric strips for binding, paper-backed fusible web, 1/2"w paper-backed fusible web tape, polyester fiberfill, four 1/2" dia. buttons, colored pencils, matte clear acrylic spray, tracing paper, graphite transfer paper, black felt-tip pen with fine point, hot glue gun, and glue sticks.

1. (*Note:* Refer to photo for all steps.) For fence appliqué, follow manufacturer's instructions to fuse web to wrong side of fence appliqué fabric. Cut four 1/2" x 6 1/4" strips from fabric for fence posts and two 1/2" x 4 1/2" strips from fabric for fence rails. For tops of fence posts, trim 1 end (top) of each 6 1/4" long fabric strip diagonally. Remove paper backing from all strips.
2. Spacing strips approx. 5/8" apart, center fence post fabric strips on pillow front fabric square with bottom ends of strips even with bottom edge of pillow front; fuse in place. Center fence rail fabric strips across fence posts approx. 2" and 4" from bottom edge of pillow front; fuse in place.
3. For borders around pillow front, fuse web tape along 1 long edge (bottom edge) on right side of 1 short border fabric strip. Remove paper backing. With right sides together and matching taped edge of border strip with top edge of pillow front, place border strip on pillow front. Fuse strip to pillow front. Press strip to right side over seam. Repeat to fuse remaining short strip

COUNTRY GARDEN PILLOW

(Continued)

to bottom edge and long strips to side edges of pillow front.

4. For bird and flowers, follow Step 4 of Feathered-Friend Pillow instructions, page 22. Use a pencil to draw additional blades of grass. Follow Step 5 of Feathered-Friend Pillow instructions to color designs, including grass.

5. For pillow and binding, follow Steps 8 - 10 of Argyle Pillow instructions, this page.

6. Hot glue buttons to fence rails.

ARGYLE PILLOW (Shown on page 18)

Note: Please familiarize yourself with *Using Fusible Products*, pages 125 - 127, before beginning this project.

For a 13" x 16½" pillow, you will need two 13" x 16½" fabric pieces for pillow front and back, a 5¼" x 16½" fabric piece for argyle panel, a 6" x 18" fabric piece for diamonds, two 1¼" x 16½" fabric strips for trim strips, two 2⅛" x 13" and two 2⅛" x 17½" fabric strips for binding, polyester fiberfill, paper-backed fusible web, ⅜"w and ½"w paper-backed fusible web tape, coordinating dimensional fabric paint in squeeze bottle with fine tip, and a chalk pencil.

1. Follow manufacturer's instructions to fuse web to wrong side of argyle panel fabric piece. Do not remove paper backing.
2. For fabric diamond shapes, leave at least 1" between shapes and trace diamond pattern 4 times onto paper side of web. Cutting approx. ½" outside drawn lines, cut out diamonds. Fuse diamonds to wrong side of diamond fabric piece; cut out diamonds along drawn lines. Remove paper backing from diamonds.

TIE PILLOW (Shown on page 18)

Note: Please familiarize yourself with *Using Fusible Products*, pages 125 - 127, before beginning this project.

For an approx. 15" square pillow, you will need two 16" squares of suit fabric for pillow front and back, 4 old neckties approx. equal in width, paper-backed fusible web, ½"w paper-backed fusible web tape, polyester fiberfill, chalk pencil, and fabric glue (if needed).

1. Use chalk pencil to draw a 4" square at center on right side of one 16" fabric square (pillow front).

3. Referring to Fig. 1, center and fuse diamonds to argyle panel fabric piece.

Fig. 1

4. Remove paper backing from panel. Center and fuse panel to 1 pillow fabric piece (pillow front).

5. For each trim strip, fuse ⅜"w web tape along 1 long edge on wrong side of 1 fabric strip. Do not remove paper backing. Press remaining long edge of strip to wrong side to meet closest edge of tape. Press taped edge to wrong side along inner edge of tape. Unfold edge and remove paper backing. Refold edge and fuse in place.

6. Fuse ⅜"w web tape along wrong side of each trim strip and remove paper backing. Center and fuse 1 trim strip over each long raw edge of argyle panel.

7. Referring to Fig. 2, use chalk pencil and a ruler to draw an "X" over each diamond on argyle panel. Use dimensional paint to paint over chalk lines; allow to dry flat.

2. Measuring from widest end, cut a 15¼" length from each tie. Following manufacturer's instructions, fuse web to wrong side of each tie. Remove paper backing.

3. (*Note:* Refer to photo for Step 3.) Matching cut edge of each tie with 1 edge of pillow front and inner edge of each tie with 1 edge of drawn square, overlap ties in a crisscross fashion on pillow front; fuse in place. If necessary, use fabric glue to secure edges of ties to pillow front; allow to dry.

4. Follow *Making a Basic Pillow*, page 127, to make pillow.

Fig. 2

8. For pillow, fuse ½"w web tape along each edge on wrong side of pillow back fabric piece. Remove paper backing. Place pillow front and back wrong sides together. Leaving an opening for stuffing along 1 edge, fuse edges together. Stuff pillow with fiberfill. Fuse opening closed.

9. For binding, follow *Making a Single Hem*, page 127, to make a ½" hem along each end of long binding strips. Use ½"w web tape and follow *Making Binding*, page 127, to make binding from all binding strips.

10. Insert 1 side edge of pillow into fold of 1 binding strip with unhemmed ends; fuse in place. Repeat to fuse remaining unhemmed binding strip to remaining side edge of pillow and hemmed binding strips to top and bottom edges.

WELCOME, LITTLE ONE!

These springtime nursery accents will make the family's newest arrival feel like "somebunny" special! With our nifty techniques, it's easy to transform floral print fabrics into a cuddly ensemble. The precious bunnies and flowers, shown off in a patchwork setting, will make baby's first room extra charming.

"Welcome" Wall Hanging, page 26

Roll out a welcome wagon full of lovable bunnies! This cute no-sew wall hanging is easily assembled using fusible web and colorful fabrics. The bunnies' faces are drawn with a felt-tip pen.

A playful combination of floral prints and easy appliqués accents nursery essentials. A smiling bunny face is fused onto the lid of a purchased jar and dressed up with a bow. For a sweet lamp, we simply gathered fabric around the base and added a little padding. The shade is adorned with glued-on fabric cutouts and edging.

Bunny Jar, page 28
Covered Lamp with Decorated Shade, page 28

Baby will love cuddling up with this snuggly comforter. It's fast and easy to machine piece, and the layers are tied with embroidery floss for an adorable quick quilt.

Quick Baby Quilt, page 29

Note: Please familiarize yourself with *Using Fusible Products, General Information*, page 125, before beginning this project.

For an approx. $15^{1}/_{4}$" x 17" wall hanging, you will need one $15^{1}/_{4}$" x 17" fabric piece for front, one $19^{3}/_{4}$" x $21^{1}/_{2}$" fabric piece for border, fabrics for appliqués and appliqué background pieces, one $3^{5}/_{8}$" x 20" fabric strip for hanging loops, 9" of $3/_{8}$"w ribbon, lightweight fusible interfacing, paper-backed fusible web, $1/_{2}$"w paper-backed fusible web tape, four $7/_{8}$" dia. buttons, embroidery floss to match border fabric, black felt-tip pen with fine point, a 17" length of $1/_{2}$" dia. wooden dowel, two $1^{1}/_{4}$" dia. wooden head beads with $1/_{2}$" dia. openings, white spray paint, liquid fray preventative, hot glue gun, and glue sticks.

1. Follow manufacturer's instructions to fuse interfacing to wrong sides of front and border fabric pieces. Follow manufacturer's instructions to fuse web to wrong side of front fabric piece.

2. Cut a $2^{1}/_{4}$" square from each corner of border fabric piece (Fig. 1).

Fig. 1

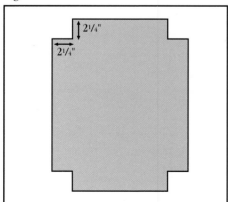

3. Remove paper backing from front fabric piece. Fuse front fabric piece to center on wrong side of border fabric piece.

4. Press top edge of border fabric piece $1/_{2}$" to wrong side. Fuse web tape along pressed edge. Do not remove paper backing. Press edge $1^{3}/_{4}$" to wrong side, covering edge of front fabric piece (Fig. 2). Unfold edge and remove paper backing. Refold edge and fuse in place. Repeat for bottom edge of border fabric piece.

Fig. 2

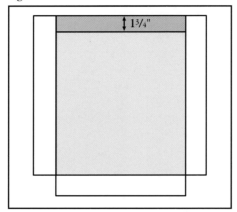

5. Press 1 corner of 1 long edge of border fabric piece diagonally (Fig. 3). Fuse web tape along pressed edge (Fig. 4). Do not remove paper backing. Repeat for remaining corners.

Fig. 3   Fig. 4

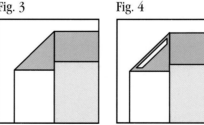

6. Press 1 long edge of border fabric piece $1/_{2}$" to wrong side. Fuse web tape along pressed edge. Do not remove paper backing. Press edge $1^{3}/_{4}$" to wrong side, covering edge of front fabric piece. Unfold edge and remove paper backing from long and diagonal edges. Refold edge and fuse in place. Repeat for remaining long edge of border fabric piece.

7. (*Note:* If using a thin fabric, follow manufacturer's instructions to fuse interfacing to wrong side of fabric before completing Steps 7 and 8. Refer to photo for Steps 7 - 13.) For appliqué background fabric pieces, fuse web to wrong sides of background fabrics. Cut a $4^{1}/_{4}$" x $8^{1}/_{2}$" fabric piece for mama bunny background, a $5^{7}/_{8}$" x $4^{1}/_{2}$" fabric piece for wheelbarrow background, and a $5^{7}/_{8}$" x $4^{1}/_{8}$" fabric piece for tulip background from fabrics.

8. For appliqués, leave at least 1" between shapes and trace patterns, pages 27, 114, and 115, indicated numbers of times onto paper side of web. Cutting approx. $1/_{2}$" outside drawn lines, cut out shapes. Follow manufacturer's instructions to fuse shapes to wrong sides of appliqué fabrics. Cut out shapes along drawn lines.

9. Remove paper backing from background fabric pieces. Overlapping edges approx. $1/_{8}$", arrange background fabric pieces on wall hanging front approx. $7/_{8}$" from bottom and side borders; fuse in place.

10. Remove paper backing from appliqués. Center letters on wall hanging front approx. 1" from top border; fuse in place. Arrange remaining appliqués on background fabric pieces, overlapping appliqués as necessary; fuse in place.

11. Use black pen to draw eyes, whiskers, mouth, and line for legs on mama bunny and eyes and whiskers on baby bunnies.

12. Tie ribbon into a bow; trim ends. Apply fray preventative to ribbon ends and allow to dry. Glue bow to mama bunny.

13. For hanging loops, follow *Making Binding*, page 127, to make binding from fabric strip. Fuse edges of binding strip together. Cut binding strip into four 5" lengths. Matching ends, fold each length in half and press. With ends extending $1/_{2}$" over top edge of wall hanging and spacing loops evenly, pin loops along top edge of

wall hanging. Use floss to sew buttons and hanging loops to wall hanging.

14. For hanging dowel, glue head beads to dowel. Paint dowel and beads white. Allow to dry. Insert dowel through hanging loops.

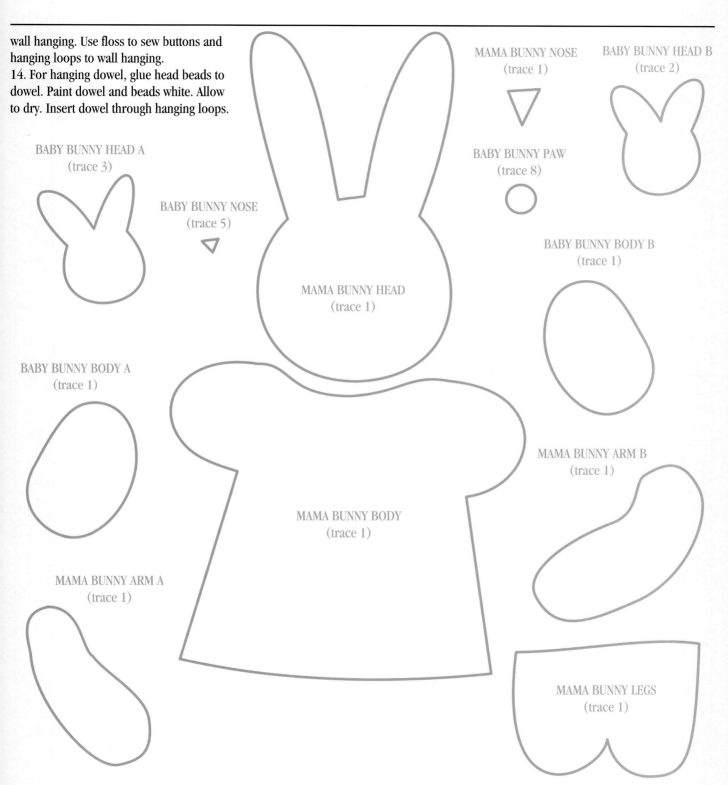

MAMA BUNNY NOSE
(trace 1)

BABY BUNNY HEAD B
(trace 2)

BABY BUNNY HEAD A
(trace 3)

BABY BUNNY PAW
(trace 8)

BABY BUNNY NOSE
(trace 5)

MAMA BUNNY HEAD
(trace 1)

BABY BUNNY BODY B
(trace 1)

BABY BUNNY BODY A
(trace 1)

MAMA BUNNY ARM B
(trace 1)

MAMA BUNNY BODY
(trace 1)

MAMA BUNNY ARM A
(trace 1)

MAMA BUNNY LEGS
(trace 1)

BUNNY JAR
(Shown on page 25)

Note: Please familiarize yourself with *Using Fusible Products*, *General Information*, page 125, before beginning this project.

You will need a quart-size Country Keeper® jar with heart-shaped lid, a 7" square of fabric for appliqué background, fabrics for appliqués, lightweight fusible interfacing (if needed), paper-backed fusible web, 9" of ³/₈"w ribbon, liquid fray preventative, black felt-tip pen with fine point, and craft glue.

1. Remove heart insert from lid. Use a pencil to draw around insert on right side of background fabric piece. Cut out heart approx. ¹/₂" outside drawn line.
2. (*Note:* If using a lightweight appliqué fabric, follow manufacturer's instructions to fuse interfacing to wrong side of fabric before completing Step 2.) For bunny appliqué, leave at least 1" between shapes and trace mama bunny head and nose patterns, page 27, onto paper side of web. Cutting ¹/₂" outside drawn lines, cut out shapes. Follow manufacturer's instructions to fuse shapes to wrong sides of appliqué fabrics. Cut out shapes along drawn lines.
3. Remove paper backing from appliqués and arrange within drawn lines of heart on background fabric piece; fuse in place.
4. Use black pen to draw eyes, whiskers, and mouth on bunny.
5. At ¹/₂" intervals, clip edges of background fabric to ¹/₁₆" from drawn lines. Center insert right side down on wrong side of background fabric. Alternating sides and pulling fabric taut, glue edges of fabric to back of insert; allow to dry.
6. Tie ribbon into a bow; trim ends. Apply fray preventative to ribbon ends and allow to dry. Glue bow to bunny; allow to dry.
7. Replace insert in jar lid. If desired, glue in place.

COVERED LAMP WITH DECORATED SHADE (Shown on page 25)

You will need a small lamp with an approx. 10" dia. shade, fabric to cover lamp base, fabrics for appliqués on shade, fabric for trim on shade, polyester fiberfill, lightweight fusible interfacing, ³/₈"w ribbon, liquid fray preventative, 12" of ¹/₄"w elastic, tracing paper, fabric glue, fabric marking pencil, string, and a thumbtack or pin.

1. To cover lamp base, refer to Fig. 1 to measure lamp from one side of neck to opposite side of neck; add 10".

Fig. 1

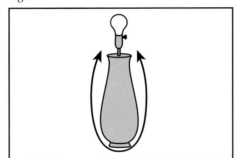

2. Cut a fabric square the measurement determined in Step 1. Fold fabric square in half from top to bottom and again from left to right. To mark cutting line, tie 1 end of string to fabric marking pencil. Measure ¹/₂ the measurement determined in Step 1 from the pencil; insert thumbtack through string at this point. Insert thumbtack through fabric as shown in Fig. 2 and mark ¹/₄ of a circle. Cut along drawn line through all layers of fabric.

Fig. 2

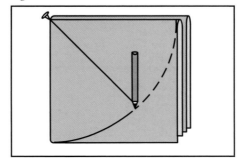

3. Center lamp on wrong side of fabric circle. Mark fabric where lamp cord extends from base of lamp. Cut a small slit in fabric at mark large enough for plug at end of cord to fit through. Apply fray preventative to raw edges of slit; allow to dry. Pull cord through slit.
4. Bring edges of fabric up loosely around neck of lamp. Place fiberfill between lamp and fabric to achieve desired fullness. Gather fabric around neck of lamp; knot elastic securely around fabric and neck of lamp (Fig. 3). Trim ends of elastic. Fold raw edges of fabric to wrong side and tuck under elastic.

Fig. 3

5. Tie ribbon into a bow around fabric, covering elastic; trim ends. Apply fray preventative to ribbon ends; allow to dry.
6. For trim along top edge of lampshade, measure around top edge of shade; add 1". Cut a 1¹/₈"w bias fabric strip the determined measurement. Press 1 end and each long edge ³/₈" to wrong side. Beginning with unpressed end at seam of shade, glue strip along top edge of shade. Repeat for trim along bottom edge of shade.
7. For appliqués on shade, follow manufacturer's instructions to fuse interfacing to wrong sides of fabrics. Trace tulip, stem, and leaves patterns, page 114, onto tracing paper; cut out. Draw around patterns indicated numbers of times on interfaced sides of fabrics. Cut out shapes. Referring to photo, glue shapes to shade, overlapping shapes as necessary.

QUICK BABY QUILT (Shown on page 25)

For an approx. 35 1/4" x 41 1/4" quilt, you will need fabrics for quilt top (see Table for amounts), a 38" x 44" fabric piece for backing, a 38" x 44" piece of high-loft polyester bonded batting, thread to coordinate with fabrics, large safety pins, and embroidery floss for ties.

Note: Refer to Diagram to assemble quilt top. For each sewing step, match right sides and raw edges and use a 1/4" seam allowance unless otherwise indicated; press seam allowances to 1 side.

1. Wash, dry, and press fabrics.
2. Referring to Table, cut pieces for quilt top from fabrics.
3. Sew piece A to piece B. Sew C to A-B. Sew D to A-B-C. Sew E to F. Sew E-F to A-B-C-D.
4. For inner top and bottom borders, sew G pieces to top and bottom of quilt top. For inner side borders, sew H pieces to sides of quilt top.
5. For outer top and bottom borders, sew I pieces to top and bottom of quilt top. For outer side borders, sew J pieces to sides of quilt top.
6. To assemble quilt, center backing fabric right side up on batting. With right sides together, center quilt top on backing. Working from center outward, smooth out any wrinkles and use safety pins to pin layers together approx. every 6". Use straight pins to pin edges of layers together.

7. Sewing 3/8" from edges of quilt top and leaving a 12" opening for turning, sew layers together. Trim seam allowance to 1/4"; trim corners.
8. Remove all pins. Turn quilt right side out. Sew final closure by hand.
9. To tie quilt, thread a needle with a 5" length of floss. Working from right side, make a small stitch through all layers where indicated by one X on Diagram. Tie ends of floss into a square knot close to fabric; trim ends to 1" from knot. Repeat for each remaining X on Diagram.

TABLE

FABRIC PIECE	SIZE	NUMBER NEEDED
A	6 1/2" x 8 1/2"	1
B	6 1/2" x 8 1/2"	1
C	12 1/2" x 8 1/2"	1
D	8 1/2" x 16 1/2"	1
E	14 1/2" x 10 1/2"	1
F	6 1/2" x 10 1/2"	1
G	20 1/2" x 3 1/2"	2
H	3 1/2" x 32 1/2"	2
I	26 1/2" x 5 1/2"	2
J	5 1/2" x 42 1/2"	2

DIAGRAM

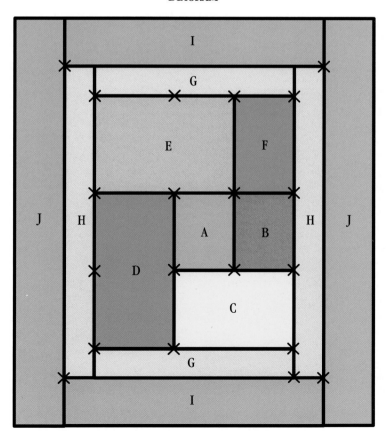

KITCHEN TOWEL CREATIONS

Bringing a fresh look to your kitchen is a breeze when you take advantage of these ideas using dish towels. Because the edges are already finished, you save lots of time! We chose coordinating towels in classic colors and patterns to create our cheery window treatments and other accents. Made for a special occasion or just a fun change, these crisp home fashions will charm your family and guests.

Café Curtains with Valance, page 34

Hung with ribbon ties, kitchen towels in an array of plaids are transformed into quaint café-style curtains before you know it! The valance is also extra-easy to make by folding each towel in half and sewing a simple casing.

The goodness of a summer garden abounds on this eye-catching wreath! The grapevine wreath is embellished with latex and freeze-dried vegetables, silk ivy, and ordinary kitchen utensils that have been antiqued. For a breezy touch, we topped the piece with a simple knotted dish towel.

Kitchen Wreath, page 34

Cheery appliqués turn plain towels into "14-carrot" kitchen helpers! They're made in no time using colorful fabric cutouts and fusible web.

Carrot-Topped Towels, page 35

Add continental flair to your cuisine by decorating with towels in kitchen-theme prints. You can hang the bistro curtain in a snap using a spring-tension rod and clip-on curtain rings. The valance is easily made by hanging several towel squares on the diagonal over a spring-tension rod.

Bistro Curtains with
Pointed Valance, page 37

Coordinating chair covers are a charming way to dress up inexpensive folding chairs. To create them, we fused cutlery motifs onto a large kitchen towel and then draped the clever cover over the back of a wooden chair. The comfy fringed cushion is sewn from a single towel and tied in place.

Complete your decor with these easy accessories for your table. Making a set of place mats couldn't be easier — just cut a kitchen towel in half and hem! A kitchen ornament glued to a raffia bow makes a cute napkin ring for the fringed fabric napkins.

Chairback Cover and Seat Cushion, page 36

Table Setting, page 37

KITCHEN WREATH
(Shown on page 31)

For a wreath that looks as fresh as a farmers' market, we started with a 14" dia. grapevine wreath; a vine of silk ivy wound around the top forms a lush backdrop for the freeze-dried lettuce and green onions, the silk garlic, and the latex carrots, radishes, artichoke, beet, and tomato, which were all hot glued to the wreath (we found our ivy and vegetables at craft stores and florist shops).

Next, we "antiqued" metal kitchen tools by spraying each item with grey primer, allowing the primer to dry, and then spraying the tools lightly and unevenly with black spray paint, Design Master® glossy wood tone spray, and Design Master® whitewash transparent glaze, allowing to dry after each coat. The kitchen tools were also hot glued to the wreath.

To coordinate our wreath with our café curtains, we topped it off with a matching "bow" created by loosely knotting a kitchen towel at its center. The "bow" was wired to the top of the wreath with florist wire.

CAFÉ CURTAINS WITH VALANCE (Shown on page 30)

For curtains, you will need a 1/2" dia. spring-tension rod, large kitchen towels (length of curtains is equal to length of towels used; we used 18" x 28" towels to make 28" long curtains), thread to match towels, 1/2"w grosgrain ribbon to match towels, and a fabric marking pencil.
For valance, you will need a 1/2" dia. spring-tension rod, large kitchen towels (length of valance is equal to 1/2 of length of towels used; we used 18" x 28" towels to make a 14" long valance), and thread to match towels.

CAFÉ CURTAINS
1. To determine placement of tension rod, measure length of 1 towel; add 1/2". Mount rod in window the determined measurement from window sill.
2. To determine number of towels needed for curtains, measure length of mounted rod; multiply by 2 1/2. Divide the determined measurement by the width of 1 towel and round up to the nearest whole number (we used 6 towels for our 42"w window). If extra fullness is desired, use additional towels.
3. For ties on each towel, match right sides and long edges and fold towel in half. Use fabric marking pencil to mark center point on 1 short edge (top) on wrong side of towel; unfold towel. Cut three 18" lengths of ribbon. Matching ends, fold each ribbon length in half; press and unfold. Position towel wrong side up with marked edge at top. With 1 ribbon length at center mark and 1 at each end of top edge of towel, center fold of each ribbon length on hem at top of towel; pin in place (Fig. 1).

Fig. 1

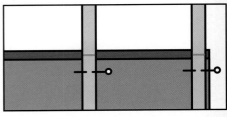

4. Using a narrow width zigzag stitch with a very short stitch length, sew across each ribbon length at fold (Fig. 2).

Fig. 2

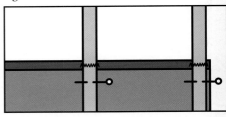

5. To hang curtains, tie ribbons into bows around rod.

VALANCE
1. To determine length of finished valance, match short edges and fold 1 towel in half; measure from fold to short edges. Allowing 1" for header, mount tension rod in window at desired height. Use a pencil to lightly mark placement of rod on window frame.
2. To determine number of towels needed for valance, measure length of mounted rod; multiply by 1 1/4. Divide the determined measurement by the width of 1 towel and round up to the nearest whole number (we used 3 towels for our 42"w window). If extra fullness is desired, use additional towels.
3. Matching wrong sides and short edges, fold each towel in half; press. Sew 1" from fold of each towel for header and 2 1/2" from fold for rod casing.
4. Remove rod from window. Insert rod into casings and hang valance.

CARROT-TOPPED TOWELS (Shown on page 31)

Note: Please familiarize yourself with *Using Fusible Products*, *General Information*, page 125, before beginning this project.

For each towel, you will need a large kitchen towel, fabrics for appliqués, paper-backed fusible web, and clear nylon thread or dimensional fabric paint in squeeze bottles to match fabrics (optional).

1. Wash and dry towel and appliqué fabrics several times to preshrink as much as possible; press.
2. For appliqués, leave at least 1" between shapes and trace carrot and carrot top patterns onto paper side of web. Cutting approx. $1/2$" outside drawn lines, cut shapes from web. Follow manufacturer's instructions to fuse shapes to wrong sides of appliqué fabrics. Cut out shapes along drawn lines.
3. Matching wrong sides and short edges, fold towel in half. Place towel on ironing board with fold at top. Remove paper backing from appliqués. With carrot overlapping carrot top approx. $1/4$", center appliqués on folded towel; fuse in place.
4. If towel will be laundered frequently, either use nylon thread and a medium width zigzag stitch with a short stitch length to stitch over raw edges of appliqués or use matching paint to paint over raw edges.
5. For laundering, follow web manufacturer's recommendations.

Note: Please familiarize yourself with *Using Fusible Products*, *General Information*, Page 125, before beginning this project.

For chairback cover, you will need a large kitchen towel at least 22" long (we used a 19" x 28¹/₂" towel to make a 19" x 14¹/₄" chairback cover), thread to match towel, an 8" x 12" piece of fabric for appliqués, paper-backed fusible web, clear nylon thread or dimensional fabric paint in squeeze bottle to match fabric (optional), and ¹/₂"w grosgrain ribbon to match towel. *For seat cushion,* you will need a large kitchen towel (we used a 19" x 28¹/₂" towel to make a 17" x 13¹/₄" seat cushion with 1¹/₂" long fringe), polyester fiberfill, thread to match towel, two 24" lengths of ¹/₂"w grosgrain ribbon to match towel, and a seam ripper.

CHAIRBACK COVER

1. For appliqués, leave at least 1" between shapes and trace utensil patterns, this page and page 37, onto paper side of web. Cutting ¹/₂" outside drawn lines, cut out shapes. Follow manufacturer's instructions to fuse shapes to wrong side of appliqué fabric. Cut out shapes along drawn lines.

2. For cover, match wrong sides and short edges and fold towel in half; place towel on ironing board with fold at top. Remove paper backing from appliqués. Arrange appliqués on folded towel; fuse in place.

3. If chairback cover will be laundered frequently, either use nylon thread and a medium width zigzag stitch with a short stitch length to stitch over raw edges of appliqués or use matching paint to paint over raw edges.

4. Hang cover over chairback and determine desired placement of side ribbons (we positioned our side ribbons approx. 11" from fold at top of cover); use pins to mark determined placement points along side edges on front and back of cover. Measure width of side of chairback at determined placement points; add 1¹/₂". Cut 2 lengths of ribbon the determined measurement. Remove cover from chair.

5. Press ends of each ribbon length ¹/₄" to 1 side (right side). At each side of cover, pin 1 pressed end of 1 ribbon length to wrong side of front and 1 end to wrong side of back at determined placement points (Fig. 1); using a wide zigzag stitch with a very short stitch length, sew ribbon ends to cover (Fig. 1).

Fig. 1

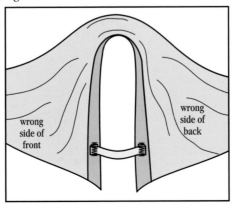

6. Turn cover right side out and slip over chairback.

SEAT CUSHION

1. Use seam ripper to remove hems from towel; press hems open.

2. Matching wrong sides and short edges, fold towel in half; press. Matching ends, fold ribbon lengths in half; press.

3. For each tie, place 2" of fold of 1 ribbon length between layers of towel at fold; pin in place (Fig. 2). Leaving an opening for stuffing, sew raw edges of towel together 1¹/₂" from edges, catching folds of ribbons in seams.

Fig. 2

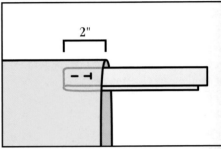

4. Lightly stuff cushion with fiberfill. Stitch opening closed.

5. Fringe raw edges of seat cushion to stitched lines.

6. Tie ribbons into bows around uprights of chairback.

BISTRO CURTAINS WITH POINTED VALANCE (Shown on page 32)

For curtains, you will need a ½" dia. spring-tension rod, large kitchen towels (length of curtains is equal to length of towels used; we used 21" x 29" towels to make 29" long curtains), and 1" dia. brass clip-on café curtain rings.

For valance, you will need a ½" dia. spring-tension rod, kitchen towels to coordinate with towels used for curtains (we used 2 sizes), and thread to match towels.

BISTRO CURTAINS

1. To determine placement of tension rod, measure length of 1 towel; add 1". Mount rod in window the determined measurement from window sill. Use a pencil to lightly mark placement of rod on window frame.

2. To determine number of towels needed for curtains, measure length of mounted rod; multiply by 2. Divide determined measurement by width of 1 towel and round up to the nearest whole number (we used 3 towels for our 30"w window). If extra fullness is desired, use additional towels.

3. Position towels on a flat surface with 1 short edge (top edge) of each towel at top and overlapping side edges of adjacent towels approx. ¼". Spacing rings evenly, clip café curtain rings along top edges of towels, clipping top corners of adjacent towels together (using 1 ring at each corner and 1 ring at center of each towel, we used 7 rings to hang 3 towels).

4. Remove rod from window. Insert rod through curtain rings and hang curtains.

POINTED VALANCE

1. To determine length of finished valance, fold 1 short edge of largest towel used to meet 1 long edge; measure from center of folded edge to folded corner (Fig. 1). Mount tension rod in window at desired height. Use a pencil to lightly mark placement of rod on window frame.

Fig. 1

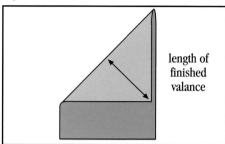

length of finished valance

2. To make a hemmed square from each towel, fold towel as shown in Fig. 1, above. Referring to Fig. 2, trim bottom from towel ½" from edge of folded corner; set aside bottom portion of towel for another use. Press raw edge of top of towel ¼" to wrong side; press ¼" to wrong side again and stitch in place.

Fig. 2

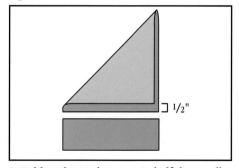

½"

3. Fold each towel square in half diagonally and press.

4. Spacing towel squares evenly, hang squares over rod, folding outer corners of end squares under to fit rod if necessary.

TABLE SETTING
(Shown on page 33)

For two place mats, you will need 1 large kitchen towel (we used a 21"x 29" towel to make two 21" x 14" place mats) and thread to match towel.

For each napkin, you will need a 15" square of fabric to coordinate with towel used for place mat and a fabric marking pencil.

For each napkin ring, you will need raffia to match napkin fabric, a miniature kitchen tool, hot glue gun, and glue sticks.

PLACE MATS

1. Matching short edges, fold towel in half; press. Unfold towel and cut in half along fold.

2. For each place mat, press raw edge of one half of towel ¼" to wrong side; press ¼" to wrong side again and stitch in place.

NAPKIN

1. Use fabric marking pencil to draw a line ¾" from each edge on wrong side of fabric square.

2. Fringe edges of napkin to drawn lines.

NAPKIN RING

1. Tie raffia into a bow around napkin.

2. Glue kitchen tool to bow.

BRIGHT IDEAS

These bright ideas will shed new light on your decor! Easy to make as well as attractive, our decorative lampshades can be created with a minimum of time and materials. They're a fun, unique way to add illuminating personality to a room.

Country Charm Lamp, page 40

Brighten the outlook of your favorite fisherman! Just transfer our fish pattern onto fabric, tint it with colored pencils, and glue the cut-out motif to the shade of a candlestick lamp. Lures, fishnet, and a raffia bow complete the outdoorsy look.

"Gone Fishin' " Lamp, page 40

This charming lamp is astonishingly easy to make by sponging gold paint onto a lampshade, gluing on gold fringe, and adding Victorian-style stickers and charms.

(Opposite) *Our delightful folk-art lamp radiates heartfelt appeal. The colorful country appliqués are fused together, embellished with simple embroidery stitches, and glued to the shade of a spool lamp.*

Charming Victorian Lamp, page 40

CHARMING VICTORIAN LAMP
(Shown on page 39)

You will need a lamp with a black lampshade with a smooth surface, metallic gold acrylic paint, small sponge piece, paper towels, Victorian-style stickers (available at specialty card shops and craft stores), assorted charms (available at craft stores), 6mm gold jump rings, 1/2"w metallic gold loop fringe, small needle-nose pliers, spring-type clothespins, matte clear acrylic spray, and craft glue.

1. To sponge-paint lampshade, dip dampened sponge piece into gold paint; remove excess paint on a paper towel. Reapplying paint to sponge as necessary, use a light stamping motion to sponge-paint shade. Allow to dry.
2. For trim along top edge of shade, measure around top edge of shade; cut a length of fringe the determined measurement. Beginning at seamline, glue fringe along top edge of shade; secure with clothespins until glue is dry. Repeat to glue fringe along bottom edge on wrong side of shade, with loops of fringe extending below edge of shade.
3. Apply stickers to shade as desired; secure with glue if necessary and allow to dry.
4. Apply 1 coat of acrylic spray to shade and allow to dry.
5. For charms, use pliers to attach 1 jump ring to eye of each charm and to 1 loop on fringe at bottom of shade, spacing charms as desired.

"GONE FISHIN'" LAMP
(Shown on page 39)

You will need a candlestick lamp with a 9" square lampshade (shade should measure at least 6" wide at center of 1 side); light green print fabric for fish (we used a light green gingham); lightweight fusible interfacing; white, pink, yellow green, blue green, dark green, and brown colored pencils; brown and black permanent felt-tip pens with fine points; tracing paper; graphite transfer paper; 2 fishing lures; an 8" x 20" strip of fishnet (available at craft stores); raffia; fabric glue; hot glue gun; and glue sticks.

1. For lampshade, follow manufacturer's instructions to fuse interfacing to wrong side of fabric. Trace fish pattern onto tracing paper. Use transfer paper to transfer pattern to right side of fabric. Use brown pen to draw over transferred lines.
2. (*Note:* Refer to photo for remaining steps.) Use colored pencils to color fish. Use black pen to draw spots on fish and to darken brown lines as desired. Cutting just outside outline, cut out fish.
3. Use fabric glue to glue fish to front of lampshade.
4. Use brown pencil to draw dashed lines to resemble stitches approx. 1/4" from top and bottom edges of shade.
5. For lamp, wrap center of fishnet strip around top of lamp base; hot glue to secure. Glue fishing lures to net. Tie raffia into a bow around lamp at top of net.

COUNTRY CHARM LAMP
(Shown on page 38)

Note: Please familiarize yourself with *Using Fusible Products*, *General Information*, page 125, before beginning this project.

You will need a spool lamp with an approx. 15" dia. lampshade; dark yellow medium weight cotton fabric for appliqué background; dark green, dark blue, dark red, and black wool fabrics or felt for appliqués; black wool fabric or felt for trim along edges of shade; paper-backed fusible web; lightweight fusible interfacing; dark yellow, green, red, dark red, and black embroidery floss; Design Master® glossy wood tone spray (optional; available at craft stores and florist shops); pinking shears; fabric marking pencil; tracing paper; embroidery needle; spring-type clothespins; and fabric glue.

1. If desired, spray lampshade lightly with wood tone spray; allow to dry.
2. Wash, dry, and press dark yellow fabric.
3. (*Note:* If using wool fabrics instead of felt, follow Step 3 to felt wool fabrics. Felting wool tightens the weave, thickens the fabric, and prevents fraying.) Machine wash wool fabrics in hot water, rinse in cold water, and dry in dryer.
4. Follow manufacturer's instructions to fuse interfacing to wrong side of dark yellow fabric. Follow manufacturer's instructions to fuse web to wrong sides of wool fabrics for appliqués.

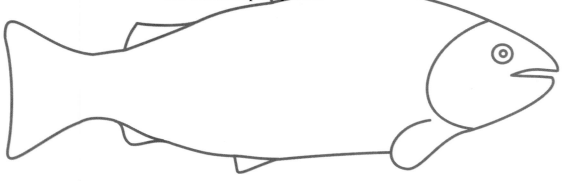

5. For patterns, follow *Tracing Patterns*, page 124.

6. For appliqué background, use pattern to cut 1 large heart from dark yellow fabric. For appliqués, use patterns to cut bird and wing from dark blue wool and leaves from dark green wool. Use pinking shears to cut small heart from black wool. For dark red heart border, use pinking shears to cut a large heart from dark red wool. Center medium heart pattern on dark red heart; use fabric marking pencil to draw around pattern. Use pinking shears to cut center from heart; discard center.

7. (*Note:* Refer to photo for remaining steps.) Remove paper backing from

appliqués. Fuse dark red heart border to dark yellow heart. Center and fuse black heart to dark yellow heart. Fuse bird, wing, and leaves to black heart.

8. (*Note:* Refer to *Embroidery* instructions, page 124, for Steps 8 and 9. Use 3 strands of floss for stitching unless otherwise indicated.) Use black floss to work *Running Stitch* along center of dark red heart border. Use green floss to work *Running Stitch* along center of each leaf; work *Blanket Stitch* along edges of leaves and *Stem Stitch* for stems on leaves. Use dark red floss to work *Blanket Stitch* along edges of bird and wing; work *Running Stitch* for line between tail feathers. Use

dark yellow floss to work *French Knot* for bird's eye. Use 6 strands of red floss to work *French Knots* for berries on black heart.

9. For trim along top edge of shade, measure around top edge of shade; add 1/2". Use pinking shears to cut a 5/8"w strip from black wool the determined measurement. Use dark yellow floss to work *Running Stitch* along center of black strip. Beginning with 1 end at seamline on shade, glue strip along top edge of shade; secure with clothespins until glue is dry. Repeat for trim along bottom edge of shade.

10. Glue appliqué to center front of shade.

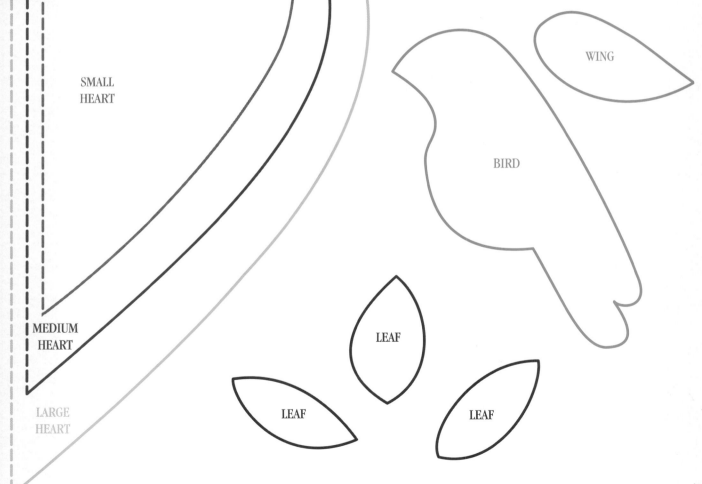

SMALL HEART

MEDIUM HEART

LARGE HEART

WING

BIRD

LEAF

LEAF

LEAF

A WORLD OF WINDOWS

Designer window treatments bring high style to any room, but who wants to pay the high price that goes with them? With our simple no-sew techniques, you can create custom-made shades, swags, and valances at a fraction of the professional cost. Just choose an array of fabrics to reflect your unique tastes — and create a bright new outlook for the windows to your world!

Elegant Swag, page 47

(Opposite) *A length of rich print fabric is simply hemmed and draped over a decorative curtain rod for an easy yet expert look.*

(Left) *Poufed in exquisite style, the formal balloon shade is gathered using quick-to-make sashes that are pinned in place.*

(Below) *Made up of individual panels, our tasseled valance lends an air of distinction to a window of any size.*

Formal Balloon Shade, page 46

Panel Valance, page 47

You can have charming window fashions by choosing bright, cheerful fabrics and accenting them with bits of springtime. A colorful balloon shade (below) *is a breeze to create by using grosgrain ribbon sashes to gather the poufs. Displayed beneath a garland of silk ivy, the crisp white valance* (opposite, top) *features a border of fused-on ribbon and silk flowers. A fun-to-make gingham swag* (opposite, bottom) *will give your windows a quick fix. All you do is hem the raw ends of the fabric, arrange the folds at the top corners, and finish it off with charming nosegays.*

Easy Balloon Shade, page 49

Appliquéd Floral Valance, page 48

Quick Window Swag, page 49

45

FORMAL BALLOON SHADE (Shown on page 43)

Note: Please familiarize yourself with *Using Fusible Products*, pages 125 - 127, before beginning this project.

You will need a 2½"w Continental® rod, medium weight fabric for shade, coordinating fabric for sashes, 1"w paper-backed fusible web tape, safety pins, and tissue paper (optional).

1. Allowing 3" for header, mount rod at window.
2. To determine width of fabric panel, measure length of mounted rod; multiply by 3. To determine length of fabric panel, measure from top of rod to window sill; add 13". Cut a piece of fabric the determined measurements, piecing with web tape if necessary.
3. Follow *Making a Double Hem*, page 127, to make a 1" hem along side edges, then bottom edge of shade. Follow *Making a Single Hem*, page 127, to make a 1" hem along top edge of shade.
4. For header and casing, fuse web tape along top edge and 4" below top edge on wrong side of shade. Do not remove paper backing. Press top edge of shade 7" to wrong side. Unfold edge and remove paper backing. Refold edge and fuse in place.
5. Remove rod from window and insert into casing; replace rod in window.
6. For sashes, measure length of shade; multiply by 1½. Cut two 5¼"w strips of fabric the determined measurement. Follow *Making a Single Hem*, page 127, to make a 1" hem along side edges and ends of each fabric strip.
7. Wrap each sash around shade with ends at top of shade behind rod; use safety pins to pin ends of sash together, gathering shade to desired length.
8. If desired, use safety pins to pin each bottom corner of shade to back of shade for added poufs. Arrange poufs in shade, stuffing lightly with tissue paper to maintain shape if desired.

MEASURING WINDOWS

Note: When measuring windows, always use a metal measuring tape; fabric tapes can sag or stretch. Measure each window individually; windows may look the same but have slightly different measurements.

Refer to Diagram to measure windows for different types of installations and lengths of window treatments. Refer to project instructions for amount to add to measurements for fullness, header, casing, or hems.

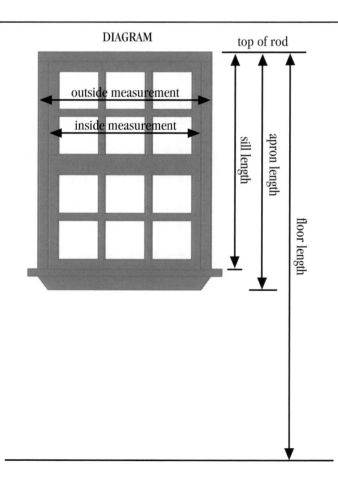

DIAGRAM

PANEL VALANCE (Shown on page 43)

Note: Please familiarize yourself with *Using Fusible Products*, pages 125 - 127, before beginning this project.

You will need a decorative wooden pole curtain rod with brackets, fabric (we used a fabric with a border pattern for our 4 panels), 1"w paper-backed fusible web tape, one 5" long tassel to coordinate with fabric for each panel, fabric marking pencil, thumbtacks, hot glue gun, and glue sticks.

1. Mount rod at window.
2. To determine number of panels needed, measure length of rod between brackets. Determine desired finished width of each panel (any number that divides evenly into rod measurement will make a good panel width; we used the stripe pattern in our fabric to help determine the width of our 10"w panels). Divide rod measurement by finished panel width and round to the nearest whole number if necessary.
3. (*Note:* Follow Steps 3 - 8 to make each panel. When making multiple panels, carefully match fabric pattern across panels.) To determine width of fabric piece for panel, add 4" to finished panel width. To determine length of fabric piece for panel, measure from top of rod to desired finished length of panel (point of panel without tassel); add 4". Cut a piece of fabric the determined measurements.
4. Follow *Making a Double Hem*, page 127, to make a 1" hem along side edges, then top edge of fabric piece.
5. Fold bottom corners of fabric piece diagonally to wrong side to form a point.

Referring to Fig. 1, use fabric marking pencil to mark a dot at bottom of point and at top of each side edge of point. Unfold fabric.

Fig. 1

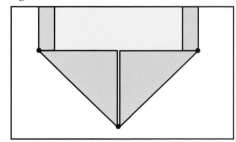

6. Fuse web tape along bottom edge of fabric piece and along each side edge from marked dot to first piece of web tape (Fig. 2).

Fig. 2

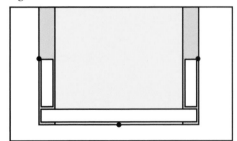

7. Remove paper backing. Fold bottom corners diagonally to wrong side again. Fuse in place.
8. Hot glue hanging loop of tassel to wrong side of panel at point.
9. For valance, drape panels over rod with 2" of top edge extending over back of rod. Use thumbtacks to secure panels in place on rod.

ELEGANT SWAG (Shown on page 42)

Note: Please familiarize yourself with *Using Fusible Products*, pages 125 - 127, before beginning this project.

You will need a decorative pole curtain rod with brackets, approx. 54"w fabric, and 1"w paper-backed fusible web tape.

1. Mount rod at window.
2. To determine length of fabric piece, drape a tape measure from 1 bracket to the other, adjusting tape measure to desired length of lower edge of swag; record measurement. Hang tape measure from 1 bracket, adjusting tape measure to desired length of cascade at each side of swag; multiply measurement by 2 and record. Add swag measurement to cascade measurement; add 4" for hems. Cut fabric the determined length.
3. Follow *Making a Double Hem*, page 127, to make a 1" hem along side edges and ends of fabric panel.
4. Centering fabric over window, drape fabric over rod, arranging fabric to achieve desired effect.

Note: Please familiarize yourself with *Using Fusible Products*, pages 125 - 127, before beginning this project.

You will need a ¹⁄₂" spring-tension rod or conventional curtain rod, medium weight white cotton fabric, paper-backed fusible web, ³⁄₈"w and 1"w paper-backed fusible web tape, silk flowers and leaves (we used pansies and ivy), ³⁄₈"w grosgrain ribbon to coordinate with flowers, dimensional fabric paint in squeeze bottle for flower centers, aluminum foil, fabric glue, yardstick, and a fabric marking pencil.

1. Allowing 2¹⁄₂" for header, mount rod in window. Use a pencil to lightly mark placement of rod in window.
2. To determine width of valance fabric piece, measure length of rod; multiply by 2. To determine length of valance fabric piece, refer to Diagram A and measure from top of rod to desired finished length of valance (our valance is 17³⁄₄" long); double measurement and add 7" for header and hems. Cut a piece of fabric the determined measurements.

3. Follow *Making a Single Hem*, page 127, to make a 1" hem along side, top, and bottom edges of fabric piece.
4. Matching wrong sides and top and bottom edges, fold fabric piece in half; press. Unfold fabric piece and lay flat with wrong side up.
5. Referring to Diagram B, fuse 1"w web tape to fabric piece for header, casing, and seams.
6. Remove paper backing; refold fabric and fuse layers together.
7. (*Note:* Follow Steps 7 - 9 to make flower appliqués.) Test petals and leaves for colorfastness by washing 1 petal and 1 leaf of each type. Use only petals and leaves that are colorfast.
8. Remove petals and leaves from stems, discarding any plastic or metal pieces. Use a warm dry iron to press petals and leaves flat.
9. Place a large piece of foil shiny side up on ironing board. Place petals and leaves

wrong side up on foil. Lay a piece of web paper side up over petals and leaves. Follow manufacturer's instructions to fuse web to wrong sides of petals and leaves. Remove paper backing. Peel petals and leaves from foil and trim excess web. Set petals and leaves aside.
10. For outer ribbon trim on valance, refer to Diagram C, page 49, and use fabric marking pencil and yardstick to draw lines on valance ³⁄₄" from each side and bottom edge; fuse ³⁄₈"w web tape along each line.
11. Cut 1 ribbon length same length as each drawn line. Fuse side ribbon lengths over web tape along side edges of valance. Trim ends of remaining ribbon length diagonally to resemble mitered corners. Fuse ribbon length over web tape along bottom edge of valance; glue ends to secure.
12. Beginning approx. ¹⁄₄" inside ribbon trim, arrange flower and leaf appliqués as desired on valance; use pressing cloth and fuse in place.

DIAGRAM A

DIAGRAM B

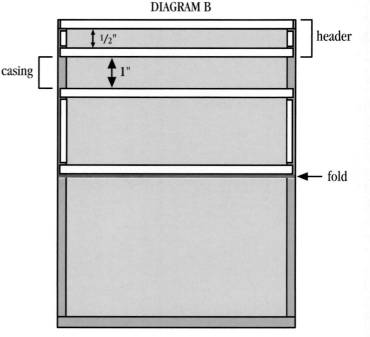

13. For inner ribbon trim, repeat Step 10, drawing lines approx. ¹/₄" from inside edges of flower appliqués. Repeat Step 11 to fuse ribbon along drawn lines.

14. Use dimensional paint to paint flower centers. Allow to dry flat.

15. Remove rod from window and insert into casing; replace rod in window.

DIAGRAM C

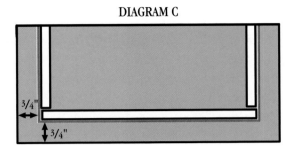

EASY BALLOON SHADE (Shown on page 44)

Note: Please familiarize yourself with *Using Fusible Products,* pages 125 - 127, before beginning this project.

You will need a ¹/₂" spring-tension rod or conventional rod, fabric, 1"w paper-backed fusible web tape, 2"w grosgrain ribbon, liquid fray preventative, safety pins (if needed), and tissue paper (optional).

1. Allowing 2¹/₂" for header, mount rod in window. Use a pencil to lightly mark placement of rod in window.
2. To determine width of fabric piece, measure length of mounted rod; multiply by 3. To determine length of fabric piece, measure from top of rod to window sill; add 10". Cut a piece of fabric the determined measurements, piecing with web tape if necessary.
3. Follow *Making a Double Hem,* page 127, to make a 1" hem along side edges, then bottom edge of panel. Follow *Making a Single Hem,* page 127, to make a 1" hem along top edge of panel.
4. For header and casing, fuse web tape along top edge and 2" below top edge on wrong side of panel. Do not remove paper backing.
5. Press top edge of panel 4¹/₂" to wrong side. Unfold edge and remove paper backing. Refold edge and fuse in place.
6. Remove rod from window and insert into casing; replace rod in window.

7. For ribbon ties, measure length of shade; multiply by 1¹/₂ and add 1 yd for bow. Cut 2 lengths of ribbon the determined measurement.
8. With center of each ribbon length at bottom of shade, tie ends of each ribbon length into a bow at top of shade, gathering shade to desired length. Trim ribbon ends.

Apply fray preventative to ribbon ends and allow to dry. If necessary, use safety pins to pin bows to shade to secure.
9. If desired, use safety pins to pin each bottom corner of shade to back of shade for added poufs. Arrange poufs in shade, stuffing lightly with tissue paper to maintain shape if desired.

QUICK WINDOW SWAG (Shown on page 45)

Note: Please familiarize yourself with *Using Fusible Products,* pages 125 - 127, before beginning this project.

You will need 45"w fabric, 1"w paper-backed fusible web tape, silk flowers (we used pansies), two 8" dia. lace doilies, assorted ribbons (we used 2 colors of silk wired ribbon and 1 color of organdy ribbon), liquid fray preventative, 2 nails, hammer, florist wire, and wire cutters.

1. Hammer 1 nail into window frame or wall at desired position of each top corner of swag, leaving approx. 1" of nail exposed.
2. To determine length of fabric piece, drape a tape measure from 1 nail to the other, adjusting tape measure to desired length of lower edge of swag; record measurement. Hang tape measure from 1 nail, adjusting tape measure to desired length of cascade at each side of swag; multiply measurement by 2 and record.

Add swag measurement to cascade measurement; add 4" for hems. Cut fabric the determined length.
3. (*Note:* If fabric has a printed selvage, follow *Making a Double Hem,* page 127, to hem selvage edges of fabric before completing Step 3.) Follow *Making a Double Hem,* page 127, to make a 1" hem along each end of fabric piece.
4. Centering fabric over window, drape fabric over nails to achieve desired effect; use wire to secure fabric to nails.
5. For each bouquet, arrange flowers and wire stems together close to flowers; trim stems to approx. 1¹/₂" from wire. Center stems of bouquet on 1 doily and gather edges of doily around flowers; use wire to secure. Tie 1 length of each type of ribbon into a bow; trim ends. Apply fray preventative to ribbon ends; allow to dry. Wire bows to bouquet. Wire bouquet to 1 end of swag.

A TOUCH OF ROMANCE

Flowers have long been reminders of romance and femininity, and with this delightful ensemble, you'll be able to bring a bit of both to your boudoir. The nightstand and clock feature lovely blooming accents and are wonderfully easy to create using paint and an effortless decoupage technique. Ordinary bottles are transformed into opulent perfume decanters when bedecked with shining trims. In practically no time, your decor will be as timeless as romance itself!

Decoupaged Night Table, page 52

Old-fashioned motifs and a poetic sentiment make this nightstand a nostalgic addition to the bedroom. For its beautiful but easy style, the unfinished table is painted white and decoupaged with pretty designs cut from gift wrap. An eloquent verse is added with a gold paint pen for a personal touch.

These embellished perfume decanters will add elegance to your dressing table. Adorned with golden trims, costume jewels, and silk flowers, the plain bottles take on a rich look that's easy — and inexpensive — to create!

Paper roses and a gilded edging give this painted timepiece a charm reminiscent of the Victorian Era. The delicate floral motifs are simply cut from printed wrapping paper and decoupaged onto the clock.

Perfume Decanters, page 52

Ornamental Clock, page 52

PERFUME DECANTERS
(Shown on page 51)

With just a little imagination and creativity, you can turn small corked glass bottles purchased from an import store and a few glittery baubles and trims into bejeweled perfume decanters. The following suggestions will help you get started.

You may need assorted acrylic jewels, desired gold ribbons and trims (we used narrow flat gold trim, scalloped fringes, gold mesh ribbons, and gold twisted cord), small silk flowers, parts of old jewelry, gold acrylic spray paint, and heavy-duty household cement.

- Remove cork from bottle and spray paint cork gold.

- Glue desired trim around top of cork.

- Glue jewels to sides of bottle or top of cork.

- Wrap ribbon around bottle, trimming to fit as necessary. Glue edges of ribbon to bottle to secure. Glue trim or cord to bottle to cover raw edges of ribbon.

- Glue jewels to ribbon or trim.

- Tie cord into a knot around bottle and fray ends.

- Glue flowers to sides or neck of bottle.

- Glue parts of old jewelry to bottle.

- Glue small jewels to centers of flowers.

ORNAMENTAL CLOCK (Shown on page 51)

You will need an unfinished wooden clock (ours measures 10" x 2" x 5½"), clock movement kit and clock hands, small motifs cut from wrapping paper, narrow flat metallic gold trim, 4 small acrylic jewels to coordinate with wrapping paper motifs, white acrylic paint, matte Mod Podge® sealer, foam brushes, fine sandpaper, tack cloth, hot glue gun, and glue sticks.

1. Sand clock; wipe lightly with tack cloth to remove dust. Allowing to dry after each coat, use foam brush to paint clock white.
2. Referring to photo, lay wrapping paper motifs on clock to determine desired placement; remove motifs from clock.

3. Use a clean foam brush to apply sealer to 1 area of clock to be decoupaged. Place motifs on clock 1 at a time and smooth in place, working from center of each motif outward. Allow to dry. Repeat to apply remaining motifs to clock.
4. Allowing to dry after each coat, use foam brush to apply 2 to 3 coats of sealer to clock.
5. Referring to photo, hot glue gold trim to clock as desired, trimming to fit. Hot glue jewels to clock at 12, 3, 6, and 9 o'clock positions.
6. Follow manufacturer's instructions to assemble and attach clock movement and hands to clock.

DECOUPAGED NIGHT TABLE (Shown on page 50)

You will need an unfinished wooden night table, motifs cut from wrapping paper, white acrylic or latex enamel paint, permanent metallic gold paint pen with fine point, metallic gold acrylic paint, spray primer and metallic gold spray paint (optional), matte Mod Podge® sealer, foam brushes, small liner and flat paintbrushes, small sponge piece, paper towels, fine sandpaper, tack cloth, tracing paper, and graphite transfer paper.

1. (*Note:* For all painting steps, allow to dry after each coat.) Remove hardware from table. Sand table; wipe lightly with tack cloth to remove dust. Use foam brush to paint table white.
2. (*Note:* Refer to photo for Steps 2 - 6.) For quotation or personal message on tabletop, cut a piece of tracing paper same size as tabletop. Use a pencil and ruler to draw guidelines for lettering on tracing paper. Trace words from quotation, page 53, onto tracing paper, spacing words as desired, or write personal message on

tracing paper. Use transfer paper to transfer words to tabletop. Use gold paint pen to paint over words.
3. Lay wrapping paper motifs on table to determine desired placement; remove motifs from table.
4. Use a clean foam brush to apply sealer to 1 area of table to be decoupaged. Place motifs on table 1 at a time and smooth in place, working from center of each motif outward. Allow to dry. Repeat to apply remaining motifs to table.
5. To sponge-paint tabletop, dip dampened sponge piece into gold acrylic paint; remove excess paint on paper towel. Use a light stamping motion to sponge-paint tabletop as desired.
6. Use paintbrushes and gold acrylic paint to paint details and trim on table as desired.
7. Allowing to dry after each coat, use a clean foam brush to apply 2 to 3 coats of sealer to table.
8. If desired, spray night table hardware with primer and then gold spray paint.
9. Replace hardware on night table.

my bounty is
as boundless as
the sea my
love as deep

SUNNY GARDEN

Bring the sunshine indoors with bold, bright sunflowers! Their vibrant petals radiate a natural feeling of warmth that's perfect for country decorating. With our brilliant garden-inspired ideas, it's easy to add lots of sunny accents to your home.

Sun-Room Curtains, page 57
Sunny Chair Pad, page 56

This cheery window treatment can be completed in an afternoon! Just use jute ties to hang lengths of muslin from a weathered stick and then twine a sunflower garland around the stick. The blooms on the chair pad are made by fusing silk petals to the muslin and painting the stems, leaves, and flower centers.

You'll have fun decorating this cheerful garden birdhouse! All you do is add a soft wash of paint and glue on bits of moss, berry garland, and silk blossoms. For a homey finishing touch, perch a little bluebird crafted from poster board near the opening.

This country watering can takes nearly no time at all to create — just paint the greenery, handle, and rim and add a silk bouquet. It'll make a cute accent for any room, especially when grouped with our decorative gardening gloves!

Garden Birdhouse, page 57

Watering Can, page 56
Gardening Gloves, page 56

WATERING CAN
(Shown on page 55)

You will need a large galvanized tin watering can, mild liquid dish soap (not lemon scented), white vinegar, green acrylic enamel paint, small flat and round paintbrushes, and desired silk flowers with leaves.

1. Wash watering can in hot soapy water; rinse well. Rinse can in a solution of 1 part vinegar and 1 part water. Dry can completely.
2. Use flat paintbrush to paint handle and handle brackets of watering can green; paint bottom rim (or an approx. 1 1/4"w band along bottom edge of can) green. Use round paintbrush to paint stems of varying heights on sides of can; paint leaves on stems. Allow to dry.
3. Arrange flowers as desired in can.

GARDENING GLOVES
(Shown on page 55)

You will need a pair of plain fabric gardening gloves, dark green fabric paint, small round paintbrush, two 12" lengths of 3-ply jute, 2 approx. 1 3/4" dia. silk flowers with stems removed, hot glue gun, and glue sticks.

1. Referring to photo and beginning at center of cuff, use paintbrush to paint stems of varying lengths on each glove; paint leaves on stems. Allow to dry.
2. Tie jute lengths into bows. Referring to photo, glue 1 bow to each glove; glue 1 flower to each glove below bow.

SUNNY CHAIR PAD (Shown on page 54)

Note: Please familiarize yourself with *Using Fusible Products, General Information,* page 125, before beginning this project.

You will need muslin, high-loft polyester bonded batting, paper-backed fusible web, silk flowers (we used approx. 3" dia. flowers), green fabric paint and desired color fabric paint for flower centers (we used dark brown for our flower centers), small round paintbrush, small sponge piece, paper towels, 3-ply jute, aluminum foil, cardboard covered with waxed paper, pressing cloth, and a large needle.

1. To determine size of muslin piece, measure seat of chair from side to side; add 2". Measure seat from back to front; double measurement and add 2". Cut a piece of muslin the determined measurements.
2. Press raw edges of muslin 1" to 1 side (wrong side). Matching wrong sides and short pressed edges, fold muslin in half; press.
3. To paint design on muslin, position muslin with fold at top and place cardboard covered with waxed paper between layers of muslin. Referring to Fig. 1, use paintbrush and green paint to paint stems of varying heights on muslin, leaving room for flowers at top; paint leaves on stems. Allow to dry.

Fig. 1

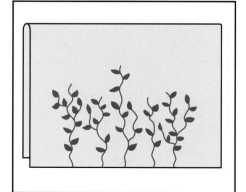

4. To fuse flowers to muslin, remove petal sections from stems, discarding any plastic or metal pieces. Use a warm dry iron to press petal sections flat.
5. Place a large piece of foil shiny side up on ironing board. Place petal sections wrong side up on foil. Lay a piece of web paper side up over petal sections. Follow manufacturer's instructions to fuse web to wrong sides of petal sections. Remove paper backing. Peel petal sections from foil and trim excess web.
6. Place muslin on ironing board. Arrange petal sections at tops of stems and cover with pressing cloth; fuse in place.
7. To sponge-paint centers of flowers, cut a small circle from sponge piece. Dip dampened sponge circle in paint for flower centers; do not saturate. Remove excess paint on a paper towel. Using a light stamping motion, use sponge circle to paint center of each flower. Allow to dry.
8. Cut a piece of batting same size as chair seat. Trim 1" from front edge and 1" from each side edge of batting. With back edge centered in fold of muslin, center batting between layers of muslin.
9. For jute stitching, thread needle with jute and use a long *Running Stitch,* page 124, to sew through all layers along front and side edges of chair pad approx. 3/4" from edges; knot and trim ends.

GARDEN BIRDHOUSE (Shown on page 55)

You will need an unfinished wooden birdhouse (ours measures 7" x 12" x 9"); brown waterbase stain; white, beige, yellow, blue, and black acrylic paint; foam brushes; small round and liner paintbrushes; 2 approx. 1/4" dia. twigs; silk flowers with leaves; sheet moss; berry garland; 12" of 3-ply jute; poster board; a 3/4" square cut from a 1/2" thick flat sponge; fine sandpaper; tack cloth; soft cloth; tracing paper; hot glue gun; and glue sticks.

1. Sand birdhouse; wipe lightly with tack cloth to remove dust.
2. Use foam brush to apply stain to birdhouse; wipe with soft cloth to remove excess stain. Allow to dry.
3. (*Note:* For remaining steps, allow paint to dry after each color.) Leaving roof unpainted and using long vertical strokes, use a clean foam brush to paint birdhouse with a mixture of 1 part white paint and 1 part water; repeat to paint house with a mixture of 1 part beige paint and 1 part water.

4. To decorate roof, measure length of 1 front edge of roof from peak to bottom; add 1". Cut twigs the determined measurement. Glue 1 twig to each front edge of roof.
5. Measure 1 front edge of roof again; double measurement. Cut a 1"w strip of moss and a length of berry garland the determined measurement. Glue moss along front edge of roof behind twigs. Glue berry garland over moss.
6. Remove several flowers and leaves from stems; glue to roof over moss and garland as desired.
7. Cutting stems desired lengths, glue several flowers to front left of birdhouse near opening. Glue a small piece of moss

over ends of stems. Tie jute into a bow; glue bow to stems of flowers above moss.
8. For bird, trace bird pattern onto tracing paper; cut out. Use pattern to cut bird from poster board.
9. Use small round paintbrush to paint bird blue. With bird facing left, use small round paintbrush to paint beak yellow. Use end of paintbrush handle to paint beige dots on side of bird and beige dot for eye. Repeat to paint a smaller black dot at center of eye. Use liner brush to paint black line along inner edge of beak.
10. Glue 1 side of sponge square to center bottom on wrong side of bird; glue remaining side to birdhouse near opening with bottom edge of bird resting on perch.

SUN-ROOM CURTAINS (Shown on page 54)

Note: Please familiarize yourself with *Using Fusible Products*, pages 125 - 127, before beginning this project.

You will need an approx. 2" dia. stick several inches longer than width of window for rod, brackets for mounting stick, muslin (we used a full width of 45"w muslin for each panel of our curtains), 1"w paper-backed fusible web tape, 3-ply jute, a large needle, wired floral garland approx. same length as stick, fabric marking pencil, hot glue gun, and glue sticks.

1. Mount brackets at window. Place stick in brackets.

2. To determine length of muslin panels for curtains, measure from bottom of mounted stick to floor; add 2". Cut 2 lengths of muslin the determined measurement.
3. Follow *Making a Single Hem*, page 127, to make a 1" hem along side edges of each panel. Follow *Making a Double Hem*, page 127, to make a 1" hem along top and bottom edges of each panel.
4. To determine number of jute ties required for each panel, measure width of panel and divide by 10; round up to the nearest whole number (we used 5 jute ties for each of our 43"w panels). Cut the determined number of 30" lengths from jute.

5. Spacing dots evenly across each panel, use fabric marking pencil to mark dots 1/2" from top edge for placement of ties.
6. Thread needle with 1 length of jute; take needle through 1 dot on panel and unthread needle. Tie ends of jute together over top edge of panel. Repeat with remaining jute lengths.
7. To hang each panel, knot ties around stick with top edge of panel hanging approx. 2" below stick.
8. Beginning at 1 bracket, loosely wrap floral garland around stick. Use glue to secure ends of garland.

COUNTRY ACCENTS

*Spreading country touches throughout your home is much easier than you think!
We've taken traditional plaids, old-timey ticking, and other rustic fabrics and combined
them to create folksy accents that you can make in a snap. Using fusible web and just
a little sewing, you'll warm up the house with down-home flair in no time!*

Country Table Skirt and Topper, page 61

Pieced Border Valance, page 61

(Above) *Enhanced with a simple pieced border, our rustic valance is held in place on a length of jute with wooden clothespins. The fabrics are joined in a flash with fusible web tape and trimmed with zigzag stitching.*

(Left) *This old-fashioned wall hanging is unbelievably easy — you quilt it as you machine piece each strip. The eye-catching appliqués are fused on and edged with long zigzag stitching.*

(Opposite) *Hearts cut from country plaids lend quaint appeal to our charming table topper. It's a cinch to create — with no sewing involved! Just use fusible web tape to hem the skirt; then tear two fabric squares for the top layers. The heartwarming motifs are fused in place and accented with "stitches" drawn with a felt-tip pen.*

Old-fashioned Wall Hanging, page 60

OLD-FASHIONED WALL HANGING (Shown on page 59)

Note: Please familiarize yourself with *Using Fusible Products, General Information,* page 125, before beginning this project.

For a 16" x 20" wall hanging, you will need fabrics for wall hanging top (see Table for amounts), a 20" x 24" fabric piece for backing (edges of backing serve as binding), one 18" x 22" piece each of muslin and low-loft cotton batting, fabrics for appliqués, a 2½" x 15" fabric strip for hanging sleeve, coordinating thread for piecing, contrasting thread for appliqué, paper-backed fusible web, and a 15" length of a ½" dia. wooden dowel.

1. Wash, dry, and press fabrics.
2. For wall hanging top, refer to Table and cut pieces from fabrics.
3. Matching edges, place batting over muslin.
4. (*Note:* Refer to Diagram for Steps 4 - 8. Use a ¼" seam allowance unless otherwise indicated.) To piece wall hanging top, center piece A right side up on batting and pin in place.
5. With right sides facing and matching 1 long edge (left edge) of B to right edge of A, place B on A; pin in place. Using coordinating thread and sewing through all layers, sew B to A along matched edges. Fold B over seam and press.
6. Repeat Step 5 to join C to B. Join D, E, F, and G in the same manner, completing center section of wall hanging top. Sew outer long edges of D and G to batting and muslin.
7. With right sides facing and matching 1 long edge (top edge) of H to bottom edge of center section, place H on center section; pin in place. Sewing through all layers, sew H to center section along matched edges. Fold H over seam and press.

8. Repeat Step 7 to join I to H. Join J, K, L, M, N, and O in the same manner. Sew outer long edges of K and O to batting and muslin.
9. Trim edges of muslin and batting even with edges of pieced fabrics.
10. (*Note:* Refer to photo for remaining steps.) Center wall hanging top right side up on wrong side of backing fabric piece; pin in place. Trim backing fabric piece to 1" larger on all sides than wall hanging top. Press short edges, then long edges of backing fabric piece ½" to wrong side. Press short edges, then long edges ½" to wrong side again, covering edges of wall hanging top; pin in place. Using contrasting thread and sewing through all layers, use a wide zigzag stitch with a long stitch length to stitch over short edges, then long edges of backing.
11. For appliqués, leave at least 1" between shapes and trace 2 hearts and 1 of each letter onto paper side of web; draw three

3½" squares on web for blocks. Cutting approx. ½" outside drawn lines, cut out shapes. Follow manufacturer's instructions to fuse shapes to wrong sides of appliqué fabrics. Cut out appliqués along drawn lines.
12. Remove paper backing from blocks, hearts, and letters and arrange on wall hanging top as desired; fuse in place.
13. Using contrasting thread and a wide zigzag stitch with a long stitch length, stitch over raw edges of hearts and blocks.
14. For hanging sleeve, press short edges then long edges of fabric strip ½" to wrong side. With wrong side of sleeve facing back of wall hanging, center sleeve on back of wall hanging ½" from top edge. Whipstitch long edges of sleeve to backing fabric.
15. Insert dowel in hanging sleeve.

DIAGRAM

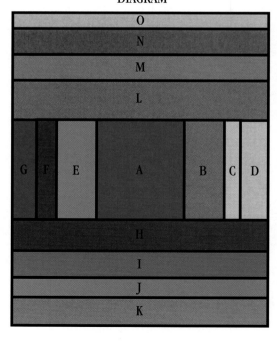

TABLE	
Fabric piece	Size (w x h)
A	6" x 7"
B	3" x 7"
C	1½" x 7"
D	2" x 7"
E	3" x 7"
F	1¾" x 7"
G	1¾" x 7"
H	16" x 2½"
I	16" x 2¼"
J	16" x 1¾"
K	16" x 2"
L	16" x 3"
M	16" x 2"
N	16" x 2¼"
O	16" x 1¼"

PIECED BORDER VALANCE (Shown on page 59)

Note: Please familiarize yourself with *Using Fusible Products*, pages 125 - 127, before beginning this project.

You will need fabrics for top section of valance and pieced border, contrasting thread for decorative stitching, 1/2"w paper-backed fusible web tape, spring-type clothespins to hang valance (we used 11 for our 66"w valance), 3-ply jute, 2 nails, hammer, and masking tape.

1. Allowing at least 2 1/2" of space above jute for clothespins, stretch jute across window at desired height and tape ends in place. At each end of jute, use a pencil to mark jute and wall or window frame where jute meets wall or window frame. Remove jute.
2. Tightly knot 1 end of jute at pencil mark. Insert nail through knot and nail to wall or window frame at pencil mark. Repeat for remaining end of jute. Trim ends of jute as desired.
3. If desired, tie several lengths of jute into a bow around each end of jute, covering nails.
4. To determine width of top section of valance, measure jute between nails; multiply by 2 1/2. To determine length of top section of valance, measure from jute to desired finished length of valance. Cut a fabric piece the determined measurements, piecing panel with web tape if necessary.
5. For pieced border, cut strips of fabric 5" wide by various lengths (we used 5 1/2" to 10" long strips).
6. To piece border, follow *Making a Single Hem*, page 127, to make a 1/2" hem along 1 short edge (side edge) of 1 border fabric strip. On right side of second strip, fuse web tape along short edge to be joined to first strip. Remove paper backing. Lay strips right side up on ironing board. Overlap hemmed edge of first strip over taped edge

of second strip. Fuse strips together. Repeat to join more strips to border until border is at least as long as top section of valance. If necessary, trim border to same length as top section.
7. To join border to top section of valance, follow *Making a Single Hem*, page 127, to make a 1/2" hem along 1 long edge (bottom edge) of top section of valance. On right side of border, fuse web tape along 1 long edge (top edge). Remove paper backing.

Lay pieces right side up on ironing board. Overlap hemmed edge of top section over taped edge of border. Fuse pieces together.
8. For decorative stitching, use a wide zigzag stitch with a long stitch length to stitch 1/4" from border on top section of valance.
9. Follow *Making a Double Hem*, page 127, to make a 1" hem along side edges, then top and bottom edges of valance.
10. Spacing clothespins evenly, use clothespins to hang valance from jute.

COUNTRY TABLE SKIRT AND TOPPER (Shown on page 58)

Note: Please familiarize yourself with *Using Fusible Products*, pages 125 - 127, before beginning this project.

For a skirt and topper for a round table, you will need fabrics for table skirt and topper, muslin and print fabrics for appliqués, paper-backed fusible web, 1"w paper-backed fusible web tape, black felt-tip pen with medium point, polyester bonded batting (optional), string, fabric marking pencil, and thumbtack or pin.

1. For table skirt, follow Steps 1 - 4 of Fringed Round Table Topper instructions, page 10, measuring table for floor length table skirt.
2. (*Note:* Refer to photo for remaining steps.) For bottom layer of table topper, follow *Measuring Tables*, page 10, to measure table for desired drop length. Tear a square of fabric the determined measurement. For top layer of table topper, tear another square of fabric 5" smaller than first square.

3. For appliqués on top layer, leave at least 1" between hearts and trace heart pattern, page 60, onto paper side of web for desired number of appliqués. Cutting approx. 1/2" outside drawn lines, cut out hearts. Follow manufacturer's instructions to fuse hearts to wrong sides of print fabrics; cut out hearts along drawn lines. Remove paper backing.
4. Fuse web to 1 side (wrong side) of muslin. Do not remove paper backing. Leaving at least 1" between hearts, fuse hearts to right side of muslin. Cutting approx. 1/4" outside hearts, cut hearts from muslin.
5. Use black pen to draw dashed lines to resemble stitching along center of muslin border around each heart.
6. Remove paper backing from hearts. Fuse hearts along edges of top layer of table topper as desired.
7. To pad table, cut a piece of batting 2" larger on all sides than tabletop. Center batting on table.
8. Center table skirt and table topper layers on table.

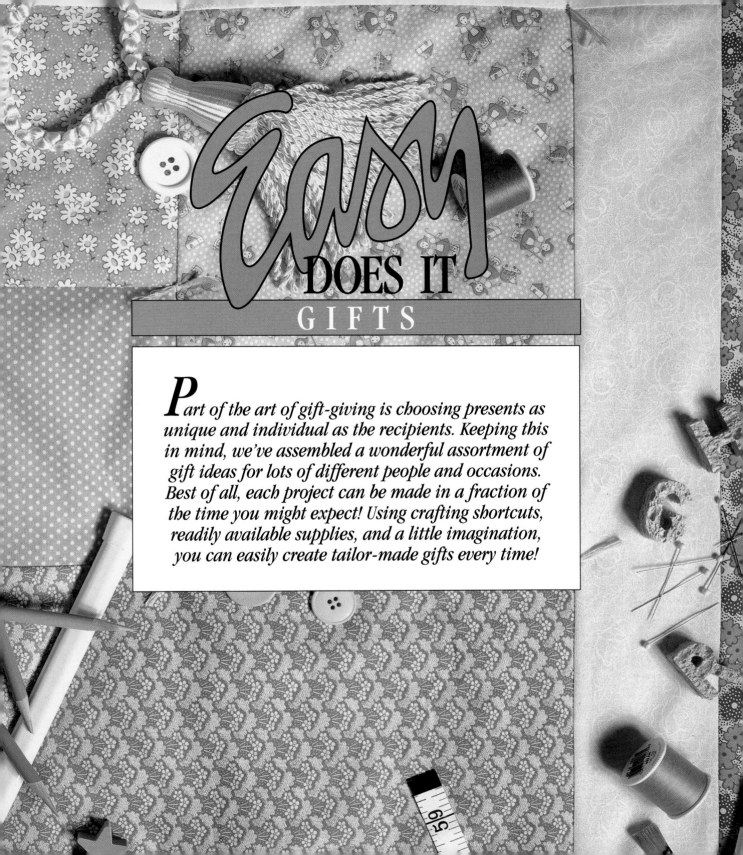

Easy
DOES IT
GIFTS

*P*art of the art of gift-giving is choosing presents as unique and individual as the recipients. Keeping this in mind, we've assembled a wonderful assortment of gift ideas for lots of different people and occasions. Best of all, each project can be made in a fraction of the time you might expect! Using crafting shortcuts, readily available supplies, and a little imagination, you can easily create tailor-made gifts every time!

SUNSHINE BEAR

*T*his darling gift will bring a ray of sunshine into anyone's heart — young or old! A purchased teddy bear becomes bonny and bright with the addition of a sunflower headband made by gluing silk flower petals along a length of bias tape. It's such a quick and super-easy craft, you'll enjoy making a cartload of these little fellows!

SUNFLOWER TEDDY

You will need a teddy bear (ours is 12"h), large silk sunflowers (we used 2 to 4 approx. 6¹/₂" dia. sunflowers), a 4" long silk leaf, brown ¹/₄"w double-fold bias tape, wire cutters, 2 small safety pins, hot glue gun, and glue sticks.

1. Remove petals from flowers; trim approx. ¹/₄" from bottom of each petal to make a straight edge. Use wire cutters to cut stem from leaf.

2. Measure around bear's head; add 14". Cut a length of bias tape the determined measurement.

3. Beginning and ending approx. 7" from ends of bias tape, glue cut edge of each petal into fold of tape, overlapping petals slightly. Glue leaf to tape behind 1 end of row of petals.

4. Wrap tape around bear's head and tie ends into a bow under chin. Use a safety pin to pin tape to each ear.

64

NEIGHBORLY WELCOME

*Y*ou'll plant seeds of friendship when you welcome new neighbors with this charming gift. An attractive yet simple idea, the sponge-painted planter is trimmed with a cordial greeting and rustic bow. Fill it with a budding plant for a gift that's truly house-warming.

"WELCOME, NEIGHBOR!" FLOWERPOT

You will need a clay pot; green, very light blue green, and light blue green acrylic paint; small sponge pieces; paper towels; Design Master® whitewash transparent glaze and glossy wood tone spray (available at craft stores and florist shops); a 2¼" x 4" piece of ivory handmade paper torn along edges and a 2½" x 4½" piece of green heavy paper for tag; brown felt-tip pen with fine point; large needle; rubber cement; and green raffia.

1. To sponge-paint rim of pot, dip a dampened sponge piece in green paint and remove excess paint on paper towel. Using a light stamping motion, use sponge piece to paint rim of pot. Allow to dry. Using a clean sponge piece for each color, repeat with light blue green and very light blue green paint.

2. Allowing to dry after each coat, spray pot with several coats of whitewash transparent glaze. Spray pot lightly with wood tone spray. Allow to dry.

3. For tag, use brown pen to write "WELCOME, NEIGHBOR!" on ivory paper piece. Glue ivory paper piece to green paper piece at an angle.

4. Tie several strands of raffia into a bow around rim of pot. Use needle to thread a strand of raffia through 1 corner of tag; tie tag to bow.

STATIONERY GIFT SET

Wonderfully easy and inexpensive, this feature-packed stationery set will delight anyone who enjoys corresponding with friends. The handy ensemble includes note cards edged using a gold paint pen and coordinating envelopes lined with wrapping paper. For the look of an expensive writing tablet, a cover of rag paper and fabric is glued onto a purchased notepad. A little spray adhesive and gift wrap turn an accordion file folder into a decorative organizer for the entire set. By choosing a wrapping paper that reflects your friend's personality, you'll deliver a gift that's letter-perfect!

For stationery file folder, you will need an accordion-style file folder, wrapping paper, lightweight cardboard, 1½"w wired ribbon, spray adhesive, hot glue gun, glue sticks, and paint pen with fine point (optional).

For notepad, you will need a plain notepad (ours measures 5" x 8"), heavy handmade paper, fabric piece for front of notepad, paper-backed fusible web, paint pen with fine point, 3/8"w ribbon, hot glue gun, and glue sticks.

For note cards, you will need plain note cards with matching envelopes, paint pen with fine point, wrapping paper, and paper-backed fusible web.

STATIONERY FILE FOLDER

1. Remove elastic strap from file folder.
2. To cover back and flap of folder, position open folder on wrapping paper. Cut a piece of wrapping paper approx. 1" larger on all sides than open folder. Apply spray adhesive to back and flap of folder. Center open folder adhesive side down on wrong side of paper piece; press firmly to secure. Trim paper even with edges of folder.
3. To cover front of folder, cut a piece of cardboard same size as front of folder. Cut a piece of wrapping paper approx. 1" larger on all sides than cardboard. Apply spray adhesive to wrong side of paper piece. Center cardboard on paper piece; press in place. Fold edges of paper to back over edges of cardboard and press in place. Hot glue covered cardboard to front of folder.
4. If desired, use paint pen to write headings on tabs inside folder.
5. Tie ribbon into a bow around folder; trim ends.

NOTEPAD

1. To determine width of paper to cover notepad, measure width of notepad. To determine length of paper to cover notepad, measure length of notepad and thickness of gummed edge. Cut a piece of handmade paper the determined measurements.
2. Matching 1 short edge of paper to bottom edge of notepad, place handmade paper on notepad. Fold top edge of paper over gummed edge of notepad; crease. Glue folded portion of paper to gummed edge of notepad.
3. Follow manufacturer's instructions to fuse web to wrong side of fabric piece. Cut fabric piece ½" smaller on all sides than top of covered notepad. Remove paper backing. Center and fuse fabric to covered notepad.
4. For label, cut a small rectangle from handmade paper. Use paint pen to write "Notes" on paper piece. Glue paper piece to center of fabric on notepad.
5. Tie ribbon into a bow around notepad; trim ends.

NOTE CARDS

1. (*Note:* Follow Steps 1 - 3 to line each envelope.) Follow manufacturer's instructions to fuse web to wrong side of wrapping paper. Do not remove paper backing.
2. Use a pencil to draw around open envelope on paper backing side of wrapping paper. Cutting just inside drawn lines, cut shape from wrapping paper. Remove paper backing.
3. Place wrapping paper piece in envelope, trimming side edges to fit if necessary; trim paper to expose gummed edge of envelope. Fuse paper to inside of envelope.
4. For each note card, use paint pen to draw a border on card to coordinate with wrapping paper.

FLORAL BASKET BOOKMARK

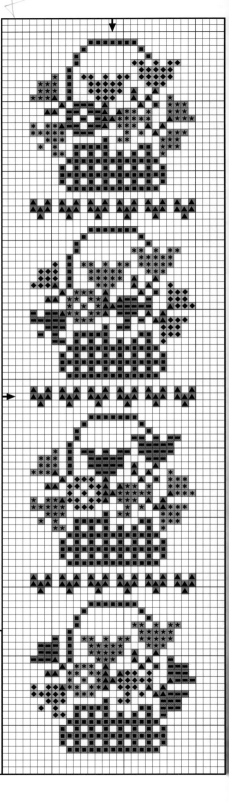

A friend who enjoys reading will appreciate the delicate spring blossoms on this pretty floral page-keeper. Cross stitched on a prefinished bookmark, the piece is especially quick and easy — even for beginners! For a thoughtful surprise, present your gift along with a popular novel.

FLORAL BASKET BOOKMARK

You will need a white Stitch-N-Mark™ bookmark (18 ct) and embroidery floss (see color key).

Center and stitch design on bookmark, using 2 strands of floss for *Cross Stitch*, page 124.

	FLORAL BASKET BOOKMARK (23w x 103h)		
X	DMC	ANC.	COLOR
■	210	108	purple
◆	353	6	peach
▲	368	214	green
★	809	130	blue
▣	840	379	brown
✳	3733	75	pink

"CHARM-ING" PURSE SET

*A*ssorted charms
*and colorful ribbon add flair
to these purchased purse
accessories. For a quick-to-
finish gift set, simply tack the
charms to the ribbon with
embroidery floss, then glue
the ribbon to each item. We
chose a Southwestern theme
for our collection, but you
can select from a variety of
ribbons and charms to create
customized designer-look
fashion accents!*

PURSE ACCESSORIES

You will need a purse accessories set,
decorative ribbon, assorted charms
(available at craft stores), embroidery floss
to match ribbon, and fabric glue.

1. (*Note:* Follow all steps for each purse
accessory. To prevent ends of ribbon from
fraying after cutting, apply fabric glue to ¼"
of ribbon around area to be cut, allow to
dry, and then cut.) Measure around section
of accessory to be decorated; add ¼". Cut
a length of ribbon the determined
measurement.
2. Use a double strand of floss to sew
charms along 1 edge of ribbon as desired.
3. Center and glue ribbon to accessory,
overlapping ends at inside or back. Allow
to dry.

GARDEN ANGEL

SEED PACKET ANGEL

Cultivate a bit of whimsy for a gardening friend with this sweet angel. Easily made by embellishing a seed packet with a wooden bead head and muslin wings, she blooms to life with silk flower accessories and a miniature spade. Hung on a doorknob or the greenhouse wall, our charming angel is sure to bring good luck during the growing season.

You will need an empty seed packet (we used a 3½" x 5½" seed packet), 1½" dia. unfinished wooden head bead, a pencil ½" longer than height of seed packet, a 9" fabric square for dress, thread to match fabric, two 4½" x 7½" pieces of muslin for wings, one 4½" x 7½" piece of fusible fleece, fabric marking pencil, heavy metallic gold thread, pink and black acrylic paint, liner and small round paintbrushes, curly doll hair, 8" long chenille stem for arms, 13" of natural twisted paper wire, 1 approx. 3" dia. silk daffodil for hat, 3 approx. ¾" dia. silk flowers with leaves for hat decoration, 1 approx. 1½" dia. silk daisy for collar, 2 approx. 1" dia. silk daffodils for cuffs, 3 approx. 1" dia. silk daisies with leaves for basket, 2"w x 2⅜"h basket with handle, 4" long spade, large needle, tracing paper, hot glue gun, and glue sticks.

1. For head and body, glue eraser end of pencil into hole in bead. Use a pencil to lightly draw eyes and mouth on bead.
2. (*Note:* Allow to dry after each paint color.) Use black paint and liner brush to paint line for mouth; use black paint and tip of paintbrush handle to paint dots for eyes. Use pink paint thinned with water and small round paintbrush to paint cheeks. Use unthinned pink paint and tip of paintbrush handle to paint hearts at corners of mouth.
3. Glue hair to top of head. Disassemble 3" dia. daffodil for hat; glue inner petal section to top of head over hair. Glue ¾" dia. flowers with leaves to front of hat.
4. For dress, trace dress pattern, page 116, onto tracing paper; cut out. Matching right sides, fold fabric square in half. Center dotted line of pattern on fold of fabric; use fabric marking pencil to draw around pattern on fabric and to mark center of neckline (indicated by X on pattern).

Cutting through both layers of fabric, cut out dress. For neck opening, cut an approx. ¼"w slit in fold of dress at center mark.
5. Using a ¼" seam allowance, sew sleeve and side seams. Clip each seam allowance where sleeve meets side. Press bottom edge of each sleeve ¼" to wrong side; baste ⅛" from each pressed edge. Turn dress right side out and press.
6. For collar, disassemble 1½" dia. daisy. Slide 1 petal section of daisy onto pencil and up against head; glue petal section to pencil. Insert pencil into neck of dress; glue neck of dress to collar.
7. For arms, insert chenille stem through sleeves. Pull basting threads to gather sleeves around ends of chenille stem, leaving ½" of each end exposed. Knot and trim ends of thread.
8. For cuffs, disassemble 1" dia. daffodils. Glue 1 inner petal section to each end of chenille stem next to sleeve.
9. For hanger, glue 1" of 1 end of twisted paper wire inside each side of seed packet.
10. Insert angel into seed packet. Bend arms forward.
11. For wings, trace wings pattern, page 116, onto tracing paper; cut out. Follow manufacturer's instructions to fuse fleece to 1 side (wrong side) of 1 muslin piece. Use fabric marking pencil to draw around pattern on 1 side (right side) of remaining muslin piece. Place muslin pieces wrong sides together; cutting through all layers, cut out wings along drawn lines. Use gold thread and *Running Stitch*, page 124, to sew layers of wings together ¼" from edges. Glue wings to back of angel and seed packet.
12. Glue remaining daisies with leaves into basket; glue basket handle to 1 arm. Glue spade to remaining hand.

A⁺ GIFTS

*S*how your appreciation for a favorite teacher with one of these brightly decorated pots. Smart gifts for any reason, they're incredibly easy to create by spray painting clay pots and then adorning them with ribbons, wooden miniatures, or sponge-painted designs. For an A+ surprise, present the clever containers filled with candies, a green plant, or even a bundle of pencils!

APPLES FOR TEACHER POT

You will need a clay pot (we used a $7^{1}/_{2}$"h pot), green spray paint, 4 approx. $1^{1}/_{2}$"h painted wooden apples and 1 apple core, $1^{2}/_{3}$ yds of $^{3}/_{8}$"w ribbon, hot glue gun, and glue sticks.

1. Allowing to dry after each coat, spray paint pot green.
2. Glue apples and apple core along rim of pot approx. $1^{1}/_{2}$" apart.
3. Cut five 12" lengths from ribbon. Tie 1 ribbon length into a bow around base of each apple and apple core; trim ends.

A-B-C POT

You will need a clay pot with saucer (we used a $4^{1}/_{4}$"h pot), white and red spray paint, ribbon same width as rim of pot, red and green acrylic paint, Miracle Sponges™ (dry compressed sponges; available at craft stores), paper towels, tracing paper, hot glue gun, glue sticks, and a black permanent felt-tip pen with medium point.

1. Allowing to dry after each coat, spray paint pot white and saucer red.
2. For ribbon trim, measure around rim of pot; add 1". Cut ribbon the determined measurement. Press 1 end of ribbon $^{1}/_{2}$" to wrong side. Beginning with unpressed end, glue ribbon around rim of pot.
3. Trace letter patterns onto tracing paper; cut out. Use black pen to draw around patterns on sponges; cut out shapes along drawn lines.
4. (*Note:* It may be helpful to practice sponge-painting on scrap paper before painting pot.) To paint letters, turn pot on side. Lightly dampen sponge shapes. Dip "A" sponge in red acrylic paint; do not saturate. Remove excess paint on a paper towel. Keeping sponge level, lightly press sponge on side of pot; carefully lift sponge. Repeat with "B" sponge and green paint and "C" sponge and red paint. Allow to dry.
5. Use black pen to outline painted letters.

"CLASS ACT" POT

You will need a clay pot (we used a $3^{1}/_{2}$"h pot), green spray paint, ribbon same width as rim of pot, an approx. 3" x 2" chalkboard ornament (available at craft stores), hot glue gun, glue sticks, and a white paint pen with fine point.

1. Allowing to dry after each coat, spray paint pot green.
2. For ribbon trim, measure around rim of pot; add 1". Cut ribbon the determined measurement. Press 1 end of ribbon $^{1}/_{2}$" to wrong side. Beginning with unpressed end, glue ribbon around rim of pot.
3. For tag, use paint pen to write "You are a class act!" on chalkboard ornament. Allow to dry. (We attached our tag to a bundle of pencils tied with ribbon.)

POT WITH "RULER" BOW

You will need a clay pot (we used a $2^{1}/_{2}$"h pot), dark red spray paint, $^{5}/_{8}$"w "ruler" ribbon, hot glue gun, and glue sticks.

1. Allowing to dry after each coat, spray paint pot dark red.
2. For ribbon trim, measure around rim of pot; add 12". Cut ribbon the determined measurement. Tie ribbon into a bow around rim of pot; trim ends. Use dots of glue to secure ribbon to pot.

PENCIL POT

You will need a clay pot (we used a $5^{3}/_{4}$"h pot), green spray paint, ribbon same width as rim of pot, sharpened pencils to fit on side of pot (we used 24 approx. $3^{1}/_{2}$" long pencils), and heavy-duty household cement.

1. Allowing to dry after each coat, spray paint pot green.
2. For ribbon trim, measure around rim of pot; add 1". Cut ribbon the determined measurement. Press 1 end of ribbon $^{1}/_{2}$" to wrong side. Beginning with unpressed end, glue ribbon around rim of pot.
3. Glue pencils to sides of pot approx. $^{3}/_{4}$" apart $^{1}/_{2}$" from bottom of pot. Allow to dry.

Whether he's a modern man or an old-fashioned guy, a special friend will love wearing a robust after-shave you've made — and you'll love the way the nostalgic scent smells on him! Just combine bay rum with spices, citrus peel, or eucalyptus to create one of our three refreshing aromas. The presentation can be tailored to his tastes, as well. Dress up a cardboard tube with an old necktie or a little greenery, or add a hand-lettered label to give your gift personalized charm.

AFTER-SHAVES

Note: Each recipe yields 1 cup (8 oz.) of after-shave; adjust recipe as needed to fill gift bottle.

For each after-shave, you will need 1 cup bay rum (available through drug stores), heat-resistant jar large enough to hold after-shave, saucepan, cheesecloth, and the following ingredients for desired scent:

SPICY AFTER-SHAVE
  $1/2$ teaspoon ground allspice
  $1/2$ teaspoon ground mace
  $1/4$ teaspoon ground cloves

CITRUS AFTER-SHAVE
  2 tablespoons dried lemon peel

EUCALYPTUS AFTER-SHAVE
  $1/4$ cup fresh or $1/8$ cup dried
       eucalyptus (undyed)
  1 lime peel, chopped

Pour bay rum and ingredients for desired scent into jar. Place jar in a saucepan filled half full with water; place pan over medium-high heat. Bring mixture in jar to a full boil for 1 minute. Remove from heat and allow to cool. Strain mixture through several layers of cheesecloth.

DECORATED GIFT BOTTLES

For each gift bottle, you will need a decorative glass bottle with cork or lid, hot glue gun, and glue sticks.
For bottle with label and bow, you will *also* need colored handmade paper, heavy ivory paper, raffia, 7" of 1"w ribbon, and a brown felt-tip pen with fine point.
For bottle with necktie wrap, you will *also* need corrugated paper (available at paper supply stores), an old necktie (we found ours at a thrift store), and a button.
For bottle in tube with greenery, you will *also* need a cardboard tube to fit around bottle, medium weight cardboard, small grapevine wreath slightly larger than diameter of tube, artificial greenery with miniature pinecones, dried mini oak, four $3^{1/2}$" lengths of jute twine, heavy ivory paper, and a brown felt-tip pen with fine point.

BOTTLE WITH LABEL AND BOW
1. For label, tear a piece of handmade paper slightly smaller than bottle front. Cut a piece of ivory paper slightly smaller on all sides than handmade paper piece.
2. Use brown pen to write "After-Shave" on ivory paper piece. Glue ivory paper piece to center of handmade paper piece. Glue label to front of bottle.
3. For bow, tie raffia lengths into a bow around neck of bottle; trim ends. Knot ribbon at center and trim ends; glue knot to raffia bow.

BOTTLE WITH NECKTIE WRAP
1. Measure bottle for desired finished height of corrugated paper. Measure around bottle; add $1/2$". Cut a piece of corrugated paper the determined measurements.
2. With corrugated side of paper facing out and overlapping edges at back, glue paper around bottle.
3. For necktie trim, measure around covered area of bottle; add 1". Cut a length from narrow part of necktie the determined measurement. Press widest end of tie length $1/2$" to wrong side. Beginning with unpressed end at front of bottle, glue necktie length around bottle.
4. Glue button to necktie trim.

BOTTLE IN TUBE WITH GREENERY
1. Measure bottle for desired finished height of tube. Cut a length from tube the determined measurement.
2. Draw around 1 end of tube on cardboard. Cut out circle just inside drawn circle. Glue cardboard circle just inside 1 end of tube (bottom). Center bottom end of tube on wreath; glue in place.
3. Glue a bundle of greenery and dried mini oak at top of tube. Knot lengths of twine together at center; glue knot to greenery bundle.
4. Cut tag shape from ivory paper. Use brown pen to write message on tag. Glue tag to tube near bundle of greenery.
5. Insert bottle in tube.

PANSY KEEPSAKE BOX

*D*ecoupage is the quick
— and incredibly easy —
technique behind this quaint
keepsake case. To beautify
the plain wooden box, it's
first painted white, then floral
motifs are cut from printed
paper napkins, arranged, and
glued in place. For a finishing
touch, attach silken blooms
to the lid, and you'll have a
thoughtful gift for a cherished
friend in no time!

DECOUPAGED KEEPSAKE BOX

You will need an unfinished wooden box
with lid (we used an 8³/₄" x 5" x 5¹/₂" box),
desired color acrylic paint, printed paper
napkin(s), silk flowers with leaves, matte
Mod Podge® sealer, foam brushes, fine
sandpaper, tack cloth, hot glue gun, and
glue sticks.

1. Sand box; wipe lightly with tack cloth to
remove dust.
2. Allowing to dry after each coat, use foam
brush to paint box desired color.
3. Unfold napkin(s). Cut desired motifs
from napkin(s) (each motif should be 1

printed layer of napkin; if necessary,
separate layers of motif).
4. Lay motifs on box to determine desired
placement; remove motifs from box.
5. Use a clean foam brush to apply sealer
to 1 area of box to be decoupaged. Place
motifs on box 1 at a time and smooth in
place, working from center of each motif

outward. Allow to dry. Repeat to apply
remaining motifs to box.
6. Allowing to dry after each coat, use foam
brush to apply 2 to 3 coats of sealer to box.
7. Remove silk flowers and leaves from
stems; hot glue flowers and leaves to front
and top of box.

PINS TO TREASURE

*O*ur elegant feminine accessories will make sweet treasures for a friend who's truly romantic at heart. Quickly fashioned using motifs cut from printed gift wrap, these easy pins are simply fused to a paper backing and coated with a shiny gloss. Dainty trims such as charms, costume jewels, and satin bows complete their fanciful look.

FLORAL PINS

For each pin, you will need floral print wrapping paper, paper-backed fusible web, tagboard (manila folder), Clear Clear Cote (a clear gloss finish for paper crafts; available at craft stores), narrow width satin ribbon, small dried flowers and greenery, a charm (available at craft stores), small acrylic jewel, pin back, liquid fray preventative, hot glue gun, and glue sticks.

1. Cutting approx. 1" outside motif, cut desired motif from wrapping paper. Follow manufacturer's instructions to fuse web to wrong side of wrapping paper piece. Remove paper backing and fuse wrapping paper piece to tagboard. Cut out motif.
2. Lay motif flat. Use a $1/4$" x 3" strip of tagboard to apply a thick coat of Clear Clear Cote to motif, being sure to bring coating to edges. Allow to dry flat 1 to 2 days.
3. Tie ribbon into a bow; trim ends. Apply fray preventative to ends and allow to dry.
4. Glue greenery, flowers, charm, bow, and jewel to motif as desired. Glue pin back to back of motif.

*F*or a special occasion or for no reason at all, show someone how much you care with one of these gorgeous topiaries! They're so easy to create, you'll want to make all three. Just take a foam ball or topiary form and cover it with miniature rosebuds, leaves, or moss and a swirl of flowers. Pretty ribbons, twining ivy, or a cluster of flowers are lovely trims. Present your friendly floral gift in a purchased decorative container, or create your own by painting a plain clay pot.

LEAF-COVERED TOPIARY TREE

You will need a 4"h clay pot; pink acrylic spray paint; metallic gold acrylic paint; small sponge piece; a 4" dia. plastic foam ball; floral foam to fit in pot; a twig for trunk; sheet moss; silk leaves to cover ball (we used approx. 65 rose leaves); assorted silk flowers with leaves; 7/8 yd of 1 1/2"w ribbon; a 1 3/4" x 4" piece of heavy ivory paper, metallic gold paint pen with fine point, and a dark pink felt-tip pen with medium point for gift card; wire cutters; paper towels; hot glue gun; and glue sticks.

1. Allowing to dry after each coat, spray paint pot pink.
2. To sponge-paint pot, dip dampened sponge piece into gold acrylic paint; remove excess paint on a paper towel. Using a light stamping motion, use sponge piece to paint pot as desired. Allow to dry.

3. For topiary form, hot glue floral foam into pot to 1/2" from rim. Hot glue sheet moss over foam, covering foam completely. For trunk, cut twig to 4" longer than desired finished height of trunk. Insert 1 end of twig 2" into foam ball; insert remaining end 2" into center of foam in pot. Use hot glue to secure trunk if necessary.
4. Use wire cutters to remove leaves from stems. Working from bottom to top of topiary ball and overlapping leaves, glue leaves to ball, covering ball completely.
5. Glue center of ribbon to top of topiary; trim ends.
6. Glue flowers and leaves to top of topiary over ribbon.
7. For gift card, use a ruler and gold paint pen to draw a border 1/4" from edges of ivory paper piece. Allow to dry. Use pink pen to write message on card. Use a small dot of hot glue to secure card to tree.

ROSE TOPIARY TREE

You will need a purchased decorative container (we used a 5" dia. x 3 1/2"h metal bucket); a topiary form with a 5" dia. foam ball top and base to fit in container; floral foam to fill remainder of container to 1/2" from rim (if needed); sheet moss; small silk roses to cover ball (we used approx. one hundred thirty-five 3/4" dia. roses); silk ivy; 2/3 yd of 1"w wired ribbon; a 1 3/4" x 4" piece of heavy ivory paper, metallic gold paint pen with fine point, and a dark pink felt-tip pen with medium point for gift card; wire cutters; hot glue gun; and glue sticks.

1. Glue base of topiary form into container. If necessary, use pieces of floral foam to fill remainder of container to 1/2" from rim; glue to secure. Glue sheet moss over foam, covering foam completely.
2. Use wire cutters to remove roses from stems. Glue roses to foam ball, covering ball completely.

3. Cut a length of ivy same length as trunk plus 4". Insert 1" of 1 end of ivy into foam ball near trunk; wind ivy around trunk. Insert remaining end of ivy into foam in pot near trunk, trimming to fit if necessary.
4. Tie ribbon into a bow; trim ends. Glue bow to trunk below foam ball.
5. For gift card, follow Step 7 of Leaf-Covered Topiary Tree instructions.

FLORAL SWAG TOPIARY TREE

You will need a 4 1/4"h clay pot; metallic gold acrylic spray paint; metallic gold acrylic paint; small sponge piece; a 9"h plastic foam cone; floral foam to fit in pot; a twig for trunk; sheet moss; dried crushed herbs and craft glue (optional); 24" long silk floral swag; three 1 1/2 yd lengths of 1/16"w satin ribbon; a 1 3/4" x 4" piece of heavy ivory paper, metallic gold paint pen with fine point, and a dark pink felt-tip pen with medium point for gift card; paper towels; hot glue gun; and glue sticks.

1. Allowing to dry after each coat, spray paint pot gold.
2. To sponge-paint pot, use liquid acrylic paint and follow Step 2 of Leaf-Covered Topiary Tree instructions.
3. For topiary form, use cone instead of ball and follow Step 3 of Leaf-Covered Topiary Tree instructions.
4. To cover cone with moss or herbs, hot glue sheet moss to cone, trimming to fit as necessary, or spread a thin layer of craft glue over cone and roll in herbs; allow to dry.
5. Beginning with 1 end of swag at top of cone and winding around cone to bottom edge, hot glue floral swag to cone, trimming to fit if necessary.
6. Tie ribbons together into a bow; trim ends. Hot glue bow to top of cone.
7. For gift card, follow Step 7 of Leaf-Covered Topiary Tree instructions.

"HOLE IN ONE" FRAME

This sporty picture frame can be made in only a few simple strokes, and it's a great gift for the golfer in your life. It's easy to create from a purchased plastic box frame — just cover the cardboard insert with fabric, glue on a coordinating trim, and add your favorite photo. Adorned with miniature golfing ornaments and a ball that's always lined up for a hole in one, it's a fun way to showcase a memory from "tee" time — or any time!

For a frame to hold an approx. 4" x 6" photo, you will need an 8½" x 11" plastic box frame with cardboard insert; fabric to cover insert; a 13½" strip cut from print fabric for border (ours measures 2½" wide); white, green, and black felt; matte gold spray paint; 10½" long wooden flagpole with flag removed; 3 approx. 5" long miniature golf clubs; plastic golf ball; golf tee; disappearing ink fabric marking pen; tracing paper; craft knife; spray adhesive; hot glue gun; and glue sticks.

1. Remove cardboard insert from frame.
2. To cover insert, use fabric marking pen to draw around insert on wrong side of fabric. Cut out fabric 1¼" outside drawn lines. Make a diagonal clip at each corner of fabric from corner to approx. ¼" from drawn lines (Fig. 1).

Fig. 1

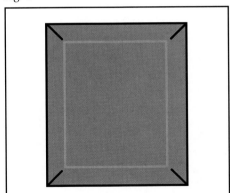

3. Apply spray adhesive to front, sides, top, and bottom of insert and reposition insert front side down on wrong side of fabric. Referring to Fig. 2, press long edges of fabric onto sides of insert; press clipped ends around corners onto top and bottom of insert. At bottom short edge of fabric, use small dots of hot glue to glue clipped ends of short edge to wrong side (Fig. 2); press short edge of fabric onto bottom of insert, using small dots of glue to glue ends in place. Repeat for top short edge of fabric.

Fig. 2

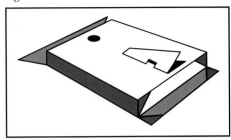

4. For border, center left long edge of print fabric strip along left front edge of insert, making sure that hanger on back of insert is at top; use dots of hot glue to glue strip in place on top and bottom of insert. If necessary, trim excess fabric along back edges of frame.
5. Apply spray adhesive to back of photograph. Center photograph approx. 3½" from top edge of insert; press in place.
6. Place insert in frame.
7. Spray paint golf clubs, flagpole, and golf tee gold; allow to dry.
8. Trace flag, "FORE," green, and hole patterns, page 117, onto tracing paper; cut out. Use patterns to cut flag and green from green felt, letters from white felt, and hole from black felt.
9. Using glue along edges only, hot glue hole to green. Cutting through both layers of felt, use craft knife to cut a small horizontal slit through center of hole and green. Hot glue green to frame, leaving slit in hole and area below slit unglued; insert bottom end of flagpole into opening in felt and hot glue flagpole to frame.
10. Hot glue letters to flag. Hot glue flag to frame next to flagpole.
11. Arrange golf clubs around photograph; hot glue in place. Hot glue golf ball and tee to green.

"GET WELL" BASKET

A basket of handmade comforts will help an ailing friend along the road to recovery. Simply use quick-and-easy no-sew methods to assemble the padded basket, tissue cover, and lozenge bag. You can complete the package with a rosy "Get Well" bookmark and an engaging best-seller for passing the time.

"GET WELL" BASKET

For padded basket, you will need a round basket with handle, fabric to cover basket, polyester bonded batting, $1/2$"w gimp trim, $1^1/2$"w decorative ribbon, large rubber band, 3 silk roses with leaves and long wired stems, wire cutters, string, fabric marking pencil, thumbtack, hot glue gun, glue sticks, and handkerchief for liner.

For covered pocket tissue, you will need an approx. $4^1/4$" x $2^1/4$" x $7/8$" tissue pack, a 6" x 8" fabric piece, 14" of $1/4$"w ribbon, small ribbon rose with leaves, hot glue gun, and glue sticks.

For a 4" x 6$5/8$" lozenge bag, you will need a 7" x 9" fabric piece, $1/2$"w paper-backed fusible web tape, 9" of $5/8$"w lace trim, 30" of $1/4$"w ribbon, and a package of lozenges to fit in bag.

For bookmark, you will need a $1^1/2$" x $7^1/4$" piece of heavy paper, metallic gold paint pen with fine point, and colored pencils.

PADDED BASKET

1. To cover basket, measure basket from 1 side of rim to opposite side of rim (Fig. 1); add 4". Cut a square of fabric the determined measurement.

Fig. 1

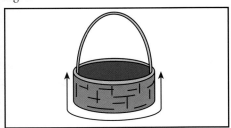

2. Fold fabric square in half from top to bottom and again from left to right. To mark cutting line, tie 1 end of string to fabric marking pencil. Measure $1/2$ the measurement determined in Step 1 from the pencil; insert thumbtack through string at this point. Insert thumbtack in fabric as shown in Fig. 2 and mark $1/4$ of a circle,

keeping pencil straight up-and-down. Cutting through all layers of fabric, cut along drawn line.

Fig. 2

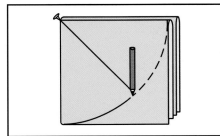

3. Draw around fabric circle on batting; cut out batting circle 1" inside drawn circle.
4. Center batting on wrong side of fabric; center basket on batting. Bring edges of fabric and batting up and hold in place with rubber band around basket rim; adjust gathers evenly. Folding raw edge of fabric to wrong side where fabric must wrap around basket handle, glue raw edge of fabric to inside of basket. Remove rubber band.
5. Glue gimp trim over raw edge of fabric, trimming to fit.
6. Tie ribbon into a bow around basket; trim ends.
7. Beginning with rose at 1 end of basket handle, twist stem of 1 rose around basket handle. Beginning with rose at opposite end of basket handle, twist stem of second rose around handle. Cut third rose from stem and glue to 1 end of basket handle.
8. Line basket with handkerchief.

COVERED POCKET TISSUE

1. Press each short edge of fabric piece $3/4$" to wrong side. Center tissue pack on wrong side of fabric piece (Fig. 3). Fold pressed edges of fabric over tissue pack, bringing edges even with edges of tissue pack opening and overlapping edges slightly at ends (Fig. 4); spot glue overlapped edges at each end to secure (indicated by X's in Fig. 4).

Fig. 3

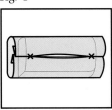

Fig. 4

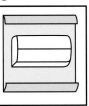

2. Fold fabric at each end of tissue pack gift-wrap style; glue to secure.
3. Beginning at center of 1 long side of pack (front), glue ribbon around sides of pack. Glue ribbon rose to pack over ribbon ends.

LOZENGE BAG

1. Follow manufacturer's instructions to fuse web tape along 1 long edge (top edge) on right side of fabric piece; do not remove paper backing. Trim $1/4$" from edge. Remove paper backing. With straight edge of lace trim overlapping web, use a pressing cloth and fuse lace along edge.
2. Fuse web tape along remaining edges on right side of fabric piece. Remove paper backing. Matching right sides and short edges, fold fabric piece in half. Fuse edges together. Turn bag right side out and carefully push corners outward, making sure seam allowances lie flat.
3. Place lozenges in bag. Tie ribbon into a bow around top of bag; trim ends.

BOOKMARK

1. Use a ruler and paint pen to draw a line approx. $1/8$" from each edge of paper piece. Allow to dry.
2. Use paint pen to write "get well wishes!" at top of bookmark. Allow to dry.
3. Use colored pencils to draw spiral circle flowers and leaves on bookmark. Use paint pen to paint dots for centers of flowers. Allow to dry.

HANDKERCHIEF BABY BONNETS

HEIRLOOM BABY BONNETS

Create an endearing keepsake for a newborn baby's christening day with one of these sweet bonnets. Each begins with a vintage handkerchief and requires only a few simple stitches. Add some ribbon, a floweret, and a bead for a loving touch. Later, the bonnet can be tucked away with the little one's other treasures. Then when baby is all grown up, just remove the stitches to create a memory-filled handkerchief for the bride — a precious "something old" for her wedding day.

For each bonnet, you will need a handkerchief (we found our approx. 11" x 12" and 13" square handkerchiefs at a local antique store), 24" of 1/4"w double-faced satin ribbon, two 4mm pearl beads, liquid fray preventative, and thread to match handkerchief and ribbons.

For cuffed bonnet, you will *also* need 30" of 1/2"w double-faced satin ribbon, two 15" lengths of 1/8"w double-faced satin ribbon for multi-loop flowerets, drawing compass, and two approx. 2" square paper pieces.

For uncuffed bonnet, you will *also* need 30" of 3/8"w double-faced satin ribbon and two 3" lengths of 3/8"w double-faced satin ribbon for gathered flowerets.

CUFFED BONNET

1. Apply fray preventative to ribbon ends to prevent fraying; allow to dry.
2. Matching wrong sides, fold handkerchief in half; press. For cuff, fold pressed edge of handkerchief approx. 1 3/4" to 1 side (right side); press.
3. For casing at back of bonnet, sew 1/4" and 3/4" from edges of handkerchief opposite cuffed edge. Thread 1/4"w ribbon length through casing. Pull ribbon ends to gather back edge of bonnet; tie ends into a bow.
4. Press ends of 1/2"w ribbon length 1/2" to 1 side. With ribbon ends tucked 1" between cuff and bonnet and stitching through all fabric layers, tack 1 pressed end of ribbon length to each front corner of bonnet.
5. (*Note:* Follow Steps 5 - 7 for each multi-loop floweret.) Use compass to draw a 1" dia. circle at center of 1 paper piece; mark center of circle. Bring threaded needle up halfway through cuff on bonnet (through 1 end of 1/2"w ribbon), through center mark on paper circle, and through 1 end of one 1/8"w ribbon length. Referring to Fig. 1, make a loop with 1/8"w ribbon with fold of loop at edge of circle; bring ribbon

down over needle to secure. Rotating circle, repeat to make 9 more loops (Fig. 2), holding floweret firmly in place.

Fig. 1

Fig. 2

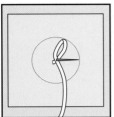

6. Stitching through center of floweret, securely tack floweret to cuff. Trim end of ribbon if necessary. Gently tear paper piece from behind floweret.
7. Sew 1 pearl bead to bonnet at center of floweret.

UNCUFFED BONNET

1. Apply fray preventative to ribbon ends to prevent fraying; allow to dry.
2. Matching wrong sides, fold handkerchief in half; press.
3. For casing at back of bonnet, sew 1/16" and 1/2" from fold. Thread 1/4"w ribbon length through casing. Pull ribbon ends to gather back edge of bonnet; tie ends into a bow.
4. Press ends of 30" ribbon length 3/8" to 1 side. With ribbon ends 1/2" from edges of bonnet and stitching through both fabric layers, tack 1 pressed end of ribbon length to each front corner of bonnet.
5. (*Note:* Follow Steps 5 - 7 for each gathered floweret.) Fold one 3" ribbon length in half and hand sew ends together; hand baste 1/16" from 1 long edge of ribbon. Pull basting thread to gather ribbon into a circle; knot and trim ends.
6. Sew floweret over ribbon end on 1 front corner of bonnet.
7. Sew 1 pearl bead to bonnet at center of floweret.

EXQUISITE WEDDING ALBUM

*H*elp a lucky couple celebrate their special day with this exquisite wedding photo album! Deceptively easy to make by covering a purchased album with fabric, the heart of its charm is a romantic frame. The elegant holder is fashioned from a purchased mat, which is lightly padded, covered with fabric, and adorned with swirls of ribbon, pearl beads, and handmade ribbon roses. Your gift can be personalized by tucking the couple's invitation inside. Later, the newlyweds can replace it with a favorite photograph from their wedding.

WEDDING ALBUM

You will need a 3-ring binder photo album, fabric to cover album, low-loft polyester bonded batting, lightweight cardboard, a wedding invitation, either a purchased mat to fit invitation and to fit on front of album or a craft knife and cutting mat or thick layer of newspapers, 5/8"w decorative ribbon, 10" of 1 1/2"w wired ribbon for bow, 2 1/2 yds of 1"w wired ribbon for wired ribbon roses, 10" of 1/2"w satin ribbon for each satin ribbon rose (we made 9 roses), 6" of 1 1/2"w lace trim with points, thread to

match ribbons and lace trim, artificial flower stamens (optional), 3mm to 6mm pearl beads, 2mm and 4mm string pearls, tweezers, hot glue gun, and glue sticks.

1. To cover outside of album, measure length (top to bottom) and width of open album. Cut a piece of batting the determined measurements. Cut a piece of fabric 2" larger on all sides than batting.

2. With album closed, glue batting to outside of album.

3. Center open album on wrong side of fabric piece. Fold corners of fabric diagonally over corners of album; glue in place. Fold short edges of fabric over side edges of album; glue in place. Fold long edges of fabric over top and bottom edges of album, trimming fabric to fit approx. 1/4" under binding hardware; glue in place.

4. To cover inside of album, cut two 2"w fabric strips 1" shorter than length (top to bottom) of album. Press ends of each strip 1/4" to wrong side. Center and glue 1 strip along each side of binding hardware with 1 long edge of each strip tucked approx. 1/4" under hardware.

5. Cut 2 pieces of cardboard 1/2" smaller on all sides than front of album. Cut 2 fabric pieces 1" larger on all sides than 1 cardboard piece. Center 1 cardboard piece on wrong side of 1 fabric piece. Fold corners of fabric diagonally over corners of cardboard piece; glue in place. Fold edges of fabric over edges of cardboard piece; glue in place. Repeat to cover remaining cardboard piece.

6. Center and glue covered cardboard pieces inside front and back of album.

7. (*Note:* For Steps 7 - 9, use purchased mat or use craft knife and cutting mat to cut desired size mat from lightweight cardboard.) For frame on front of album, use a pencil to lightly draw around mat and mat opening on wrong side of fabric. Cutting 1" from drawn lines, cut out fabric shape (Fig. 1); at corners of opening in fabric, clip fabric to 1/8" from drawn lines.

Fig. 1

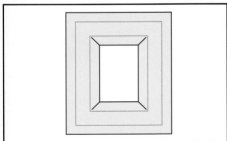

8. Use mat as a pattern to cut a piece of batting. Glue batting to mat. Center mat batting side down on wrong side of fabric. Fold fabric edges at opening of mat to back; glue in place. Fold corners of fabric diagonally over corners of mat (Fig. 2); glue in place. Fold remaining fabric edges to back of mat; glue in place.

Fig. 2

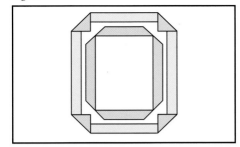

9. Center frame on front of album; leaving an opening at top for invitation, glue sides and bottom of frame to album.

10. Measure around outer edges of frame. Cut a length of 4mm string pearls the determined measurement. Glue pearls along outer edges of frame, trimming to fit (leave opening for invitation at top).

11. Cut a length of 5/8"w decorative ribbon twice the total length around frame. Loosely knot ribbon approx. every 3". Beginning at center top of frame and loosely twisting ribbon, spot glue ribbon along center of each side of frame, trimming to fit. Drape 2mm string pearls loosely along ribbon, threading pearls through loops and knots in ribbon. Spot glue pearls in place, trimming to fit.

12. For bow, cut an 8" length and a 2" length of 1 1/2"w wired ribbon. Overlapping ends 1", form a loop from 8" length and tack ends together; flatten loop with overlap at center. Wrap 2" ribbon length around center of loop; tack in place. Glue bow to top of frame, covering ends of ribbon and pearl trim.

13. Cut two 3" lengths of lace trim. Baste 1/8" from straight edge of each length. Pull basting threads to gather straight edge of each length; knot threads and trim ends. Glue 1 gathered lace length to frame behind each side of bow.

14. For wired ribbon roses (on and around bow), cut two 18" lengths and two 27" lengths from 1"w wired ribbon. Follow Steps 1 - 4 of Wired Ribbon Rose Pins instructions, page 93, to make 1 rose from each ribbon length. Glue large roses to bow and small roses below bow.

15. (*Note:* Follow Steps 15 and 16 to make desired number of satin ribbon roses to decorate frame.) For each rose, fold 1 end of one 10" ribbon length diagonally to meet 1 long edge (bottom edge) of ribbon (Fig. 3). To form center of rose, tightly roll folded portion of ribbon (Fig. 4); stitch at bottom to secure.

Fig. 3   Fig. 4

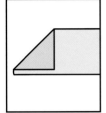   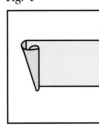

16. To form petals, fold top edge of ribbon to back as shown in Fig. 5. Roll rose center toward folded section until all of folded section is wrapped around center; stitch at bottom to secure. Fold top edge of ribbon to back again (Fig. 6). Continue rolling, stitching, and folding until end of ribbon is 2" to 3" long. Trim end of ribbon to 1/2". Fold end diagonally to back of rose and stitch in place.

Fig. 5   Fig. 6

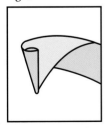   

17. Glue ribbon roses along twisted ribbon on frame.

18. Glue a pearl bead to center of each rose on frame.

19. Insert invitation in frame.

SPORTSMAN'S THROW

You warm my heart. Love, Clara

CAMOUFLAGE PILLOW AND THROW

This handsome afghan and pillow are perfect for your sportsman's favorite chair — and they're so simple to make! The throw can be completed in minutes by cutting fringe on a piece of fleece, and the fused-on heart-shaped tag bears a thoughtful message. The matching welted pillow is surprisingly fast and simple to sew as well. Whether he's braving a night in the woods or watching the Monday night game, this sporty afghan and pillow set will keep him warm and cozy.

Note: If making heart appliqué tag, please familiarize yourself with *Using Fusible Products, General Information,* page 125, before beginning this project.

For an approx. 18" square pillow, you will need a 20" x 40" piece of camouflage-print deep-pile polyester fleece, a $2^1/2$" x 2 yd bias fabric strip (pieced as necessary) and 2 yds of $^3/8$" dia. cord for welting, thread to match welting fabric, and polyester fiberfill.
For an approx. 60" x 72" throw, you will need 2 yds of 60"w camouflage-print deep-pile polyester fleece, chalk pencil, and a yardstick.
For heart appliqué tag for throw, you will need one 7" square each of muslin and print fabric, paper-backed fusible web, pinking shears, and a permanent felt-tip pen with fine point.

PILLOW
1. Wash and line dry fleece.
2. For welting, press 1 end of bias fabric strip $^1/2$" to wrong side. Center cord on wrong side of bias strip. Matching long edges, fold strip over cord. Using zipper foot, baste along length of strip close to cord; trim seam allowance to $^1/2$".
3. Cut two 18" squares from fleece for pillow front and back. Beginning at center bottom and matching raw edges, pin welting to right side of 1 pillow fabric square, overlapping ends of welting. Baste welting in place, clipping seam allowance at corners. Remove basting from ends of welting as necessary, trim cord to fit where ends meet, and overlap pressed end of welting fabric

over unpressed end of welting fabric; baste ends in place.
4. Matching right sides, place pillow fabric squares together. Sewing as close as possible to welting and leaving an opening for turning, use zipper foot to sew raw edges together. Clip corners and turn right side out. Stuff pillow with fiberfill. Sew final closure by hand.

THROW
1. Wash and line dry fleece. If necessary, trim selvages from fleece.
2. Use chalk pencil and yardstick to draw a line 5" from each short edge of fabric. Cutting from edge of fleece to drawn line, make cuts approx. $^1/4$" to $^3/8$" apart to make fringe along each short edge.

HEART APPLIQUÉ TAG FOR THROW
1. Wash, dry, and press fabric pieces.
2. Trace heart pattern onto paper side of web. Cutting approx. $^1/2$" outside drawn lines, cut out heart. Follow manufacturer's instructions to fuse heart to 1 side (wrong side) of muslin square. Use pinking shears to cut heart from muslin.
3. Fuse web to wrong side of print fabric square. Do not remove paper backing. Remove paper backing from muslin heart; center and fuse heart to print fabric square. Cutting approx. $^1/2$" from muslin heart, use pinking shears to cut heart from print fabric.
4. Use permanent pen to write message on heart.
5. Remove paper backing from heart; fuse to throw as desired.

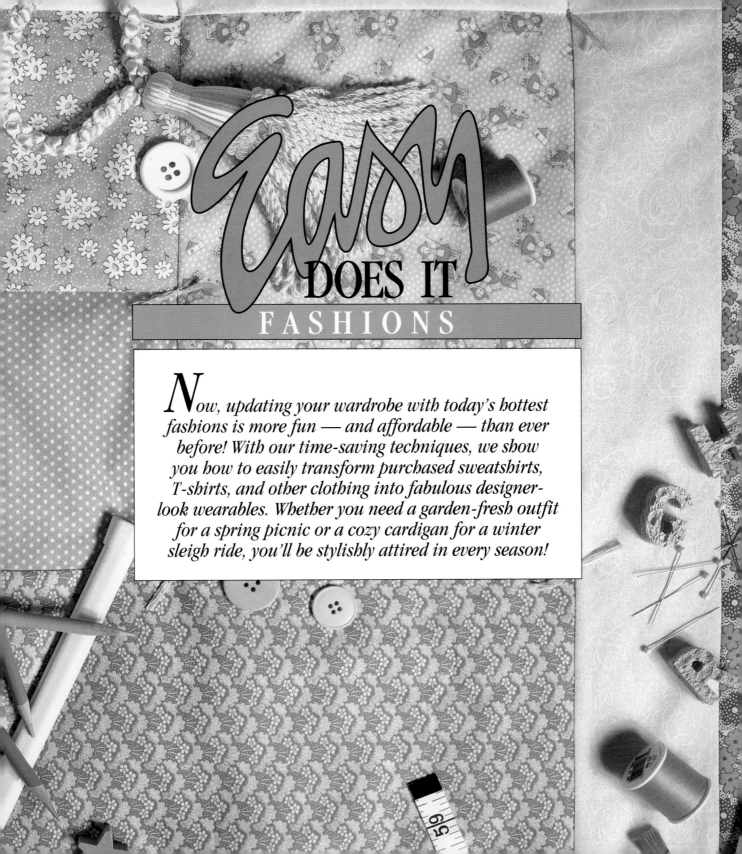

Easy

DOES IT

FASHIONS

*N*ow, *updating your wardrobe with today's hottest fashions is more fun — and affordable — than ever before! With our time-saving techniques, we show you how to easily transform purchased sweatshirts, T-shirts, and other clothing into fabulous designer-look wearables. Whether you need a garden-fresh outfit for a spring picnic or a cozy cardigan for a winter sleigh ride, you'll be stylishly attired in every season!*

QUICK RIBBON ROSES

WIRED RIBBON ROSE PINS

These ribbon roses will lend elegance to any outfit — and because you make them yourself, you won't have to pay expensive boutique prices! Great for perking up a jacket, hat, or blouse, these pins are quick and super-easy to make. You simply gather and coil wired ribbon, stitching it in place as you go. Add ribbon leaves or a bow to create an instantly beautiful boutonniere!

For each rose pin, you will need 1¹/₂"w wired ribbon for rose (²/₃ yd for small rose or 1 yd for large rose); either 22" of 1"w green wired ribbon for rose with bow (light yellow rose), two 6" lengths of 2"w green wired ribbon for rose with leaves (dark yellow rose), or 22" of 1¹/₂"w green wired ribbon for rose with gathered ribbon circle (burgundy rose); green wired ribbon for backing; thread to match ribbon for rose; artificial flower stamens (optional); lightweight cardboard; drawing compass; tweezers; large pin back; liquid fray preventative; hot glue gun; and glue sticks.

Note: Apply fray preventative to all ribbon ends; allow to dry.

1. Gather 1 long edge (bottom edge) of ribbon for rose by gently pulling wire from both ends with tweezers and pushing ribbon toward center.

2. To form center of rose, fold 1 end of ribbon diagonally to meet bottom edge (Fig. 1). Fold ribbon end again (Fig. 2); roll ribbon end tightly 2 to 3 times and stitch at bottom to secure (Fig. 3).

Fig. 1

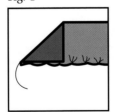

Fig. 2

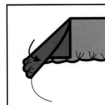

Fig. 3

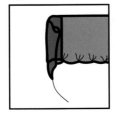

3. If stamens are desired, place stamens on ribbon next to rose center; glue in place.

4. To form petals, continue to roll ribbon loosely around center, with bottom edge winding slightly upward and stitching bottom edge in place as you go. At end of ribbon, fold end of ribbon diagonally to back of rose and stitch in place. Clip ends of excess wire to approx. ¹/₂" from rose; bend each end to 1 side.

5. For rose with bow, tie 22" length of 1"w green ribbon into a bow; trim ends. Glue bow to back of rose.

6. For each leaf on rose with leaves, match ends and fold one 6" green ribbon length in half. Glue ends of ribbon to back of rose.

7. For rose with gathered ribbon circle, gather 1 long edge (bottom edge) of 22" length of 1¹/₂" w green ribbon by gently pulling wire from both ends with tweezers and pushing ribbon toward center. Bring ends of ribbon together and overlap to form a circle. Fold each end of ribbon diagonally to center of circle; glue in place. Clip ends of excess wire to approx. ¹/₂" from ribbon; bend each end to 1 side. Glue gathered circle to back of rose.

8. For backing, use compass to draw a 1³/₄" dia. circle for small rose or a 2³/₈" dia. circle for large rose on cardboard; cut out circle. Cover 1 side (front) of cardboard circle with lengths of green ribbon, gluing ribbon ends to back of circle. Glue back of covered circle to back of rose; glue pin back to covered circle.

ROSY SHIRT

*C*elebrate the beauty
of spring all year long with
this flowery chambray
shirt! Just cut the roses from
print fabric, fuse them
on, and edge them with
dimensional fabric paint
for a pretty look that's super-
simple. The herringbone
"stitches" on the placket
and cuffs are also painted.
This rosy top will be a lovely
addition to any wardrobe.

FLORAL APPLIQUÉD SHIRT

Note: Please familiarize yourself with *Using Fusible Products, General Information*, page 125, before beginning this project.

You will need a long-sleeved shirt with cuffs, floral print fabric, paper-backed fusible web, dimensional fabric paint in squeeze bottles to match fabric and for "stitching" on shirt, small sharp scissors, tracing paper, graphite transfer paper, and a T-shirt form or cardboard covered with waxed paper.

1. Wash, dry, and press shirt and appliqué fabric according to web and paint manufacturers' recommendations.
2. Follow manufacturer's instructions to fuse web to wrong side of fabric. Use scissors to cut flower and leaf motifs from fabric. Remove paper backing from motifs and arrange on shirt; fuse in place.

3. Insert T-shirt form into shirt. Allowing to dry after each color, use matching paint to paint over outlines and raw edges of motifs.
4. For decorative "stitches," trace stitch pattern onto tracing paper; use transfer paper to transfer design onto placket of shirt between buttonholes and onto cuffs. Use desired paint color to paint over transferred lines; allow to dry.
5. To launder, turn shirt wrong side out and follow web and paint manufacturers' recommendations; hang to dry.

FLOWER FUN VEST

*A*dd a little fun to your wardrobe with this snazzy springtime vest. It's a snap to decorate with simple fabric cutouts and colorful buttons. Adorned with plaid tulips and button-centered daisies, this easy-to-make accessory is a whimsical way to give new life to an old denim vest or add pizzazz to a new one!

FLOWER FUN VEST

Note: Please familiarize yourself with *Using Fusible Products*, *General Information*, page 125, before beginning this project.

You will need a denim vest, fabrics for appliqués, paper-backed fusible web, clear nylon thread or dimensional fabric paint in squeeze bottles to match fabrics (optional), two 1¹/₄" dia. white buttons, decorative ladybug button, decorative buttons to replace buttons on vest, and thread to match buttons.

1. Wash, dry, and press vest and appliqué fabrics according to web manufacturer's recommendations.
2. For flower and leaf appliqués, leave at least 1" between shapes and trace 1 of each daisy, 2 tulips, and 4 leaves, page 118, onto paper side of web. Cutting approx. ¹/₂" outside drawn lines, cut out shapes. Follow manufacturer's instructions to fuse shapes to wrong sides of fabrics for flowers and leaves; cut out shapes along drawn lines. Remove paper backing from shapes.

3. Arrange flowers on vest as desired.
4. For stems, fuse web to wrong side of fabric for stems. To determine length of strip(s) to cut for each stem, measure from center of each flower to bottom of vest. If stem will lie over false pocket, measure from center of flower to bottom of inside of false pocket and from top of false pocket to bottom of vest. To end stem in false pocket, just measure to bottom of inside of false pocket. Cut a ¹/₂"w fabric strip for each determined measurement.
5. Remove paper backing from stems and position on vest with tops under flowers. Fuse flowers and stems in place.

If necessary, trim stems even with bottom edges of vest.
6. Arrange leaves along stems as desired; fuse in place.
7. If vest will be laundered frequently, either use nylon thread and a medium width zigzag stitch with a short stitch length to stitch over raw edges of appliqués or use dimensional paint to paint over raw edges.
8. Sew one 1¹/₄" white button to vest at center of each daisy, sew ladybug button to 1 leaf, and replace buttons on vest.
9. To launder, turn vest wrong side out and follow web manufacturer's recommendations; hang to dry.

*T*he flowers on this summertime tee are fast, fun, and very easy to make — just stencil on simple shapes and add accents with paint and a marker! To create the unique waffle-patterned bloom, place a piece of plastic canvas under the T-shirt before stenciling. For added charm, trim the sleeves with buttons and tie up one side of the hem with a pretty bow.

SIMPLE STENCILED SHIRT

You will need a T-shirt; yellow, green, and dark pink fabric paint; acetate for stencils; craft knife; cutting mat or thick layer of newspapers; a 6" square of 7 mesh plastic canvas; small flat sponge pieces; six 7/8" dia. white buttons; embroidery floss to match dark pink paint; paper towels; removable tape; T-shirt form or cardboard covered with waxed paper; black permanent felt-tip pen with medium point; and 1 1/2 yds each of 5/8"w and 7/8"w ribbon to coordinate with paint colors and liquid fray preventative (optional).

1. Wash, dry, and press shirt according to paint manufacturer's recommendations. Insert T-shirt form into shirt.
2. For each stencil, cut a piece of acetate 1" larger on all sides than pattern. Center acetate over pattern and use permanent pen to trace pattern onto acetate. Use craft knife and cutting mat to cut out shapes along drawn lines, making sure edges are smooth; discard cutouts, saving acetate circle from center of flower.

3. (*Note:* Follow Steps 3 and 4 for each flower on shirt. For flower stenciled with waffle pattern, place plastic canvas piece under front of shirt before stenciling flower.) Place flower stencil on shirt; use a small roll of tape to tape acetate circle from center of flower to shirt at center of flower stencil.
4. Hold or tape flower stencil in place. Dip 1 flat side of a clean, lightly dampened sponge piece into dark pink paint; do not saturate. Remove excess paint on a paper towel; sponge must be almost dry for best results. Beginning at edge of cut-out area, use a stamping motion to apply paint. For darker colored flower, repeat. Carefully remove stencils and allow to dry.
5. Using green paint for leaves and yellow paint for flower centers and buds, repeat Step 4 to stencil leaves, flower centers, and buds on shirt as desired.

6. To paint green shading between stenciled shapes, dip a sponge piece in green paint; do not saturate. Remove excess paint on a paper towel. Use a light stamping motion to stamp green paint on shirt.
7. If necessary, follow manufacturer's instructions to heat-set paint.
8. Use permanent pen to draw around stenciled shapes on shirt; draw veins on leaves and stems and vines on shirt as desired.
9. To cuff each sleeve, fold sleeve hem up 2 to 3 times. Use floss to sew 3 buttons approx. 1 1/2" apart along front of each cuff.
10. If desired, gather bottom of shirt at 1 side and tie ribbons into a bow around gathered part of shirt; trim ends of ribbons. Apply fray preventative to ribbon ends and allow to dry.
11. To launder, remove ribbons, turn shirt wrong side out, and follow paint manufacturer's recommendations; hang to dry.

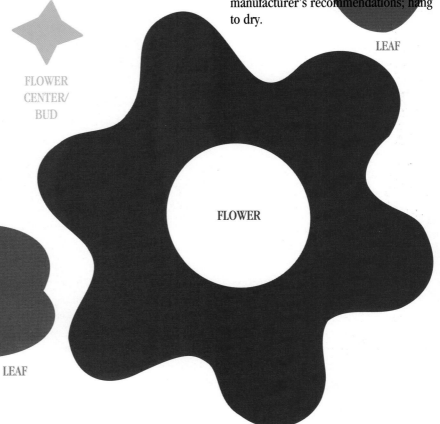

FLOWER CENTER/ BUD

LEAF

LEAF

FLOWER

SILKY SPRING PETALS

*Y*ou won't need April showers to "grow" the blooms on this pretty springtime shirt. It's amazingly simple to make — just fuse silk flower petals onto a T-shirt, outline the edges with dimensional paint, and presto! You have a seasonably stylish top that's perfect for gathering flowers or going on a picnic in the park with friends.

SPRINGY APPLIQUÉ SHIRT

Note: Please familiarize yourself with *Using Fusible Products*, *General Information*, page 125, before beginning this project.

You will need a T-shirt, assorted silk flowers and leaves, dimensional fabric paint in squeeze bottles with very fine tips to coordinate with silk flowers and leaves, paper-backed fusible web, aluminum foil, pressing cloth, and a T-shirt form or cardboard covered with waxed paper.

1. Wash, dry, and press shirt according to web and paint manufacturers' recommendations. Test petals and leaves for washability by washing 1 petal and 1 leaf of each type. Use only petals and leaves that are colorfast.
2. Remove petals and leaves from stems, discarding any plastic or metal pieces. Use a warm dry iron to press petals and leaves flat.

3. Place a large piece of foil shiny side up on ironing board. Place petals and leaves wrong side up on foil. Lay a piece of web paper side up over petals and leaves. Follow manufacturer's instructions to fuse web to wrong sides of petals and leaves. Remove paper backing. Peel petals and leaves from foil and trim excess web.
4. Arrange petals and leaves as desired around neckline on front of shirt and cover

with pressing cloth. Fuse petals and leaves to shirt.
5. Insert T-shirt form into shirt. Use dimensional paint to paint over raw edges of petals and leaves and to paint details as desired. Allow to dry.
6. To launder, turn shirt wrong side out and follow web and paint manufacturers' recommendations; hang to dry.

PRETTY EASY TEE

*C*elebrate the beauty of nature with this blossoming wreath. Created by simply fusing silk flower petals to a T-shirt, it's a great way to enjoy the splendor of a garden. We detailed the edges with dimensional paint and pinned on a pretty bow for a finishing touch. What a lovely accent for your warm-weather wardrobe!

FLORAL WREATH SHIRT

Note: Please familiarize yourself with *Using Fusible Products, General Information,* page 125, before beginning this project.

You will need a T-shirt, assorted silk flowers and leaves, dimensional fabric paint in squeeze bottles with very fine tips to coordinate with flowers and leaves, several ⅓ yd lengths of satin ribbon to coordinate with silk flowers, paper-backed fusible web, aluminum foil, pressing cloth, liquid fray preventative, T-shirt form or cardboard covered with waxed paper, and a safety pin.

1. Wash, dry, and press shirt according to web and paint manufacturers' recommendations. Test petals and leaves for washability by washing 1 petal and 1 leaf of each type. Use only petals and leaves that are colorfast.

2. Remove petals and leaves from stems, discarding any plastic or metal pieces. Use a warm dry iron to press petals and leaves flat.

3. Place a large piece of foil shiny side up on ironing board. Place petals and leaves wrong side up on foil. Lay a piece of web paper side up over petals and leaves. Follow manufacturer's instructions to fuse web to wrong sides of petals and leaves. Remove paper backing. Peel petals and leaves from foil and trim excess web.

4. Arrange petals and leaves in a circle on front of shirt and cover with pressing cloth. Fuse petals and leaves to shirt.

5. Insert T-shirt form into shirt. Use dimensional paint to paint over raw edges of petals and leaves and to paint details as desired. Allow to dry.

6. Tie ribbon lengths into a bow; trim ends. Apply fray preventative to ribbon ends; allow to dry. Use safety pin on wrong side of shirt to pin bow to shirt at bottom of wreath.

7. To launder, turn shirt wrong side out, remove bow, and follow web and paint manufacturers' recommendations; hang to dry.

COZY QUILT-BLOCK SWEATSHIRT

*D*ressed up with floral quilt-block motifs in autumn hues, this cozy sweatshirt gives a new twist to an old craft. It couldn't be easier to make — the quilt-block pieces are simply cut out and fused in place! Buttons add the finishing touches for a contemporary look that's warm with nostalgia.

EASY AUTUMN QUILT-BLOCK SWEATSHIRT

Note: Please familiarize yourself with *Using Fusible Products, General Information,* page 125, before beginning this project.

You will need a sweatshirt with set-in sleeves (sweatshirt should measure at least 19" wide across front), fabrics for appliqués, paper-backed fusible web, three 5/8" dia. buttons, thread to match buttons, tracing paper, and clear nylon thread or dimensional fabric paint in squeeze bottles to match fabrics (optional).

1. Wash, dry, and press sweatshirt and appliqué fabrics according to web manufacturer's recommendations.
2. Follow manufacturer's instructions to fuse web to wrong sides of fabrics. Do not remove paper backing.
3. For appliqué patterns, draw a 4 1/2" square, a 2 1/4" square, and a 1" square on tracing paper. Trace flower, flower center, and leaf patterns onto tracing paper. Cut out patterns.

4. For appliqués, cut a 6 1/2" x 17 1/2" piece from 1 appliqué fabric for background. Use patterns to cut the following shapes from fabrics: three 4 1/2" squares for blocks, six 2 1/4" squares for triangles on blocks, eight 1" squares for connecting squares, 3 flowers, 3 flower centers, and 12 leaves. Cut each 2 1/4" square in half diagonally. Do not remove paper backing from shapes.
5. Remove paper backing from 1" squares and 4 1/2" squares. Using 1" squares for spacing, position 1" squares and 4 1/2" squares on background fabric piece.
6. Remove paper backing from 2 1/4" triangles. Referring to Fig. 1, place one 2 1/4" triangle in each corner of each 4 1/2" square. Fuse shapes in place.

Fig. 1

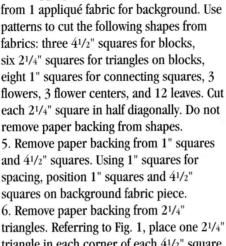

7. Remove paper backing from flowers, flower centers, and leaves. Arrange 4 leaves, 1 flower, and 1 flower center on each 4 1/2" square; fuse in place.
8. Remove paper backing from background fabric piece. Center appliquéd panel on sweatshirt approx. 1 1/2" below neckline; fuse in place.
9. If sweatshirt will be laundered frequently, either use nylon thread and a medium width zigzag stitch with a short stitch length to stitch over raw edges of appliqués or use dimensional paints to paint over raw edges.
10. Sew 1 button to each flower on shirt.
11. To launder, turn shirt wrong side out and follow web manufacturer's recommendations; hang to dry.

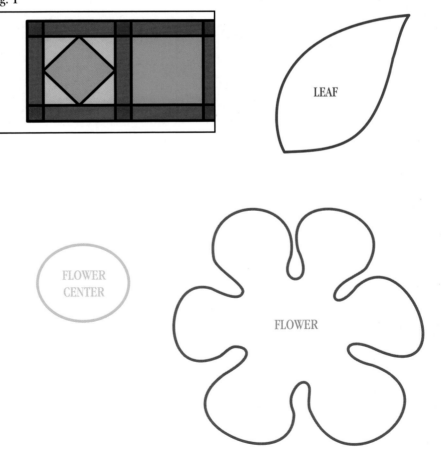

LEAF

FLOWER CENTER

FLOWER

BON VOYAGE TOP AND TOTE

Ahoy, mateys! This seaworthy set will have you shipshape for traveling in no time! The nautical flags, cut from an assortment of colorful ribbons, are easy to attach with fabric glue. In just the time it takes to dry, you'll have a cute look that's sure to hold up in fresh or salty breezes.

For top, you will need a cotton pullover shirt with waistband, 10" of 1¹/₂"w and 1¹/₂" of ³/₈"w grosgrain ribbon for bow, T-shirt form or cardboard covered with waxed paper, and a safety pin.

For tote, you will need a large canvas tote bag (ours is 21"w x 15"h), 1¹/₂"w grosgrain ribbon for trim at top of tote, and 12" of 1¹/₂"w and 1¹/₂" of ³/₈"w grosgrain ribbon for bow.

You will also need ³/₈"w grosgrain ribbon and several 2¹/₂" lengths of 1¹/₂"w grosgrain ribbon for string of flags (we used 7 different ribbons for flags), removable tape, spring-type clothespins, liquid fray preventative, and fabric glue.

TOP

1. Wash, dry, and press shirt according to glue manufacturer's recommendations. Insert T-shirt form into shirt.

2. For string of flags, measure diagonally from center of left shoulder seam to top of waistband at right side of shirt; subtract 4". Cut a length of ³/₈"w ribbon the determined measurement. Cut a V-shaped notch in 1 end of ribbon. With straight end at center of left shoulder seam, arrange ribbon across shirt as desired; secure ends with tape.

3. For flags, cut a V-shaped notch in 1 end of each 2¹/₂" ribbon length. With straight end of each flag under ³/₈"w ribbon length, arrange flags on shirt approx. 1" apart; glue straight end of each flag in place. Remove tape from ³/₈"w ribbon and glue ribbon to shirt over straight ends of flags; allow to dry.

4. For bow, overlap ends of 1¹/₂"w ribbon length 1" to form a loop; glue overlapped ends together. Flatten loop with overlap at center; pinch center of loop to gather. Wrap ³/₈"w ribbon length around center of loop and glue ends at back of bow, trimming to fit if necessary; use clothespins to secure bow until glue is dry.

5. Use safety pin on wrong side of shirt to pin bow to shirt at shoulder seam.

6. Carefully apply fray preventative to ribbon ends only; allow to dry.

7. To launder, turn shirt wrong side out, remove bow, and follow glue manufacturer's recommendations; hang to dry.

TOTE

1. For string of flags, measure diagonally from top right corner to bottom left corner of tote; subtract 2". Cut a length of ³/₈"w ribbon the determined measurement. Cut a V-shaped notch in 1 end of ribbon. With straight end at upper right corner, arrange ribbon across tote as desired; secure ends with tape.

2. For flags, follow Step 3 of Top instructions.

3. For trim, measure around top of tote; add 1". Cut a length of 1¹/₂"w ribbon the determined measurement. Press 1 end of ribbon length ¹/₂" to wrong side. Beginning with unpressed end at seamline, glue ribbon along top edge of tote; use clothespins to secure ribbon until glue is dry.

4. For bow, follow Step 4 of Top instructions. Glue bow to tote.

5. Carefully apply fray preventative to ribbon ends only; allow to dry.

LIL' SWEETHEART SHIRT

*Y*our favorite little sweetheart will be the prettiest girl on the block in this adorable top. It's easy to make by sweetening a T-shirt with hearts, buttons, and rickrack. All you need is a little fusible web and some fabric glue, dimensional paint, and other basic craft items. What a lovable way to celebrate Valentine's Day — or any day!

SWEETHEART SHIRT

Note: Please familiarize yourself with *Using Fusible Products, General Information,* page 125, before beginning this project.

You will need a child's red T-shirt, three 7" squares of red print fabrics for hearts, three 6½" squares of paper-backed fusible web, white rickrack, 12" of ¼"w red satin ribbon for bow, assorted red and white buttons, red embroidery floss, white dimensional fabric paint in squeeze bottle with very fine tip, child's T-shirt form or cardboard covered with waxed paper, small safety pin, liquid fray preventative, and fabric glue.

1. Wash, dry, and press shirt and fabrics according to web and paint manufacturers' recommendations.
2. Trace heart pattern, page 119, onto paper side of each web square. Follow manufacturer's instructions to fuse 1 web square to wrong side of each fabric square; cut out hearts along drawn lines. Remove paper backing.

3. Arrange hearts on shirt; fuse in place.
4. Insert T-shirt form into shirt. Measure shirt front from side to side. Cut 2 lengths of rickrack the determined measurement. Apply fray preventative to ends of rickrack; allow to dry. Glue 1 length of rickrack across shirt approx. 1" above and 1 length approx. 1" below hearts. Allow to dry flat.
5. Use dimensional paint to paint small dots ⅛" to ¼" apart along edges of hearts. Allow to dry flat.

6. Use embroidery floss to sew buttons to hearts as desired.
7. Tie ribbon into a bow; trim ends. Apply fray preventative to ribbon ends; allow to dry. Use safety pin on wrong side of shirt to pin bow to 1 heart.
8. To launder, turn shirt wrong side out, remove bow, and follow web and paint manufacturers' recommendations; hang to dry.

COZY CARDINAL SWEATER

*K*eep cheery and warm when cool weather comes with this fast-and-easy cardinal sweater. It's cute, it's comfortable, and it takes virtually no time to make. Just by appliquéing fabric cutouts onto a purchased cardigan and adding details with simple embroidery stitches, you can create this fashionable sweater for your wardrobe — and still have time to feed the birds!

CARDINAL CARDIGAN

Note: Please familiarize yourself with *Using Fusible Products, General Information,* page 125, before beginning this project.

You will need a cotton cardigan sweater, fabrics for appliqués, lightweight fusible interfacing (if needed), paper-backed fusible web, tracing paper, and black floss and floss to match beak fabric.

1. Wash, dry, and press sweater and appliqué fabrics according to web and sweater manufacturers' recommendations.
2. (*Note:* If using a thin fabric, follow manufacturer's instructions to fuse interfacing to wrong side of fabric before completing Step 2.) Follow manufacturer's instructions to fuse web to wrong sides of fabrics.
3. Trace cardinal and birdhouse patterns, pages 120 and 121, onto tracing paper; cut out.

4. For appliqués, use patterns to cut indicated numbers of shapes from fabrics.
5. Remove paper backing from appliqués. Referring to Diagram, page 120, and overlapping appliqués as necessary, arrange appliqués on sweater; fuse in place.
6. (*Note:* Refer to *Embroidery* instructions, page 124, for Step 6.) Use 4 strands of floss to match beak fabric to work *Blanket Stitch*

along edges of beaks; make a *French Knot* for each bird's eye where indicated by dot on mask pattern. Use 4 strands of black floss to work *Blanket Stitch* along raw edges of remaining appliqués.
7. To launder, turn sweater wrong side out and follow web and sweater manufacturers' recommendations; hang to dry.

*T*his charming appliquéd sweater is a snap to make — just cut the vase and flower shapes from your favorite fabrics, fuse them onto a purchased sweater, and blanket stitch along the edges! The bow is attached with a safety pin and can be easily removed for laundering. Abloom with beauty, this top will bring a breath of spring to a winter day!

APPLIQUÉD WINTER NARCISSUS

Note: Please familiarize yourself with *Using Fusible Products, General Information,* page 125, before beginning this project.

You will need a cotton sweater, fabrics for appliqués, paper-backed fusible web, lightweight fusible interfacing (if needed), embroidery floss to coordinate with fabrics, 2/3 yd of 1 1/2"w grosgrain ribbon, liquid fray preventative, and a large safety pin.

1. Wash, dry, and press sweater and appliqué fabrics according to web and sweater manufacturers' recommendations.
2. (*Note:* If using a thin fabric, follow manufacturer's instructions to fuse interfacing to wrong side of fabric before completing Step 2.) For appliqués, leave at least 1" between shapes and trace flowerpot, rim, 8 flowers, 8 flower centers, and 4 buds onto paper side of web. Cutting approx. 1/2" outside drawn lines, cut out shapes. Follow manufacturer's instructions to fuse shapes to wrong sides of fabrics. Cut

out shapes along drawn lines. Remove paper backing from shapes.
3. With rim overlapping slightly over flowerpot and leaving approx. 2 1/2" between bottom flowers and rim, arrange appliqués as desired on sweater; fuse in place.
4. Use 3 strands of coordinating floss to work *Blanket Stitch,* page 124, along raw edges of appliqués.

5. Tie ribbon into a bow; trim ends. Apply fray preventative to ribbon ends; allow to dry. Use safety pin on wrong side of sweater to pin bow to sweater between flowers and flowerpot.
6. To launder, turn sweater wrong side out, remove bow, and follow web and sweater manufacturers' recommendations; hang to dry.

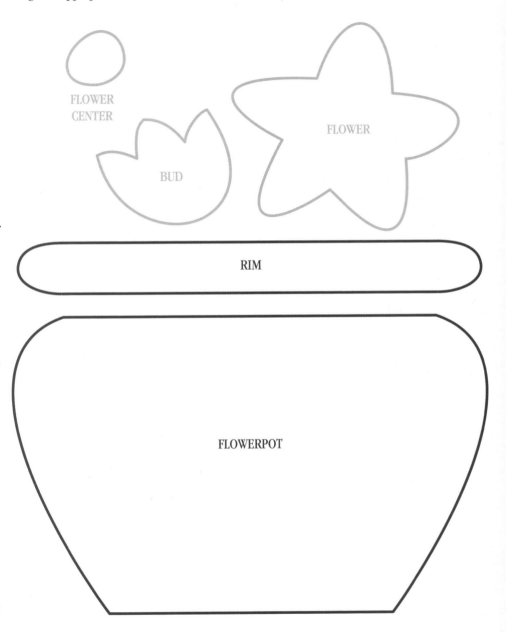

FLOWER CENTER

BUD

FLOWER

RIM

FLOWERPOT

PUMPKIN PATCH FUN

A favorite child can romp around the pumpkin patch in style with this appliquéd sweatshirt. Paper-backed fusible web makes it easy to cut and apply the fabric shapes, which you then enhance with paint, raffia, and buttons. This whimsical shirt will be so much fun for a youngster to wear — and so little effort for you to make!

PUMPKIN PATCH SWEATSHIRT

Note: Please familiarize yourself with *Using Fusible Products, General Information,* page 125, before beginning this project.

You will need a child's sweatshirt, fabrics for appliqués, paper-backed fusible web, natural Darice® Straw Satin Radiant Raffia Straw, red fabric paint and small round paintbrush for cheeks, two ¼" dia. black buttons and black thread for eyes, clear nylon thread or dimensional fabric paint in squeeze bottles to match fabrics (optional), large needle, and a black permanent felt-tip pen with fine point.

1. Wash, dry, and press sweatshirt and appliqué fabrics according to web manufacturer's recommendations.
2. For appliqués, leave at least 1" between shapes and trace patterns, page 122, indicated numbers of times onto paper side of web. Cutting approx. ½" outside drawn lines, cut out shapes. Follow manufacturer's instructions to fuse shapes to wrong sides of fabrics. Cut out shapes along drawn lines.

3. Remove paper backing from appliqués. Overlapping appliqués as necessary, arrange appliqués on sweatshirt front; fuse in place.
4. If shirt will be laundered frequently, either use nylon thread and a medium width zigzag stitch with a short stitch length to stitch over raw edges of appliqués or use matching paint to paint over raw edges.
5. For scarecrow face, use black pen to draw mouth. Use paintbrush and red paint

to paint small circles for cheeks; allow to dry. Sew buttons to face for eyes.
6. For each scarecrow hand and foot, thread large needle with an 8" length of raffia straw. Working from right side, make a small stitch through sweatshirt. Unthread needle and knot ends of raffia straw close to sweatshirt; trim ends to 1" from knot.
7. To launder, turn shirt wrong side out and follow web and raffia straw manufacturers' recommendations; hang to dry.

CELESTIAL TEE

*S*imple stars and crescent moons inspire out-of-this-world designs for summer apparel! A bright gold T-shirt is the ideal backdrop for our celestial silhouettes, made in just minutes by using dots of brilliant blue paint to fill in the moon outlines and radiate out from the stars. Adding a few acrylic jewels will give your heavenly creation an extra twinkle.

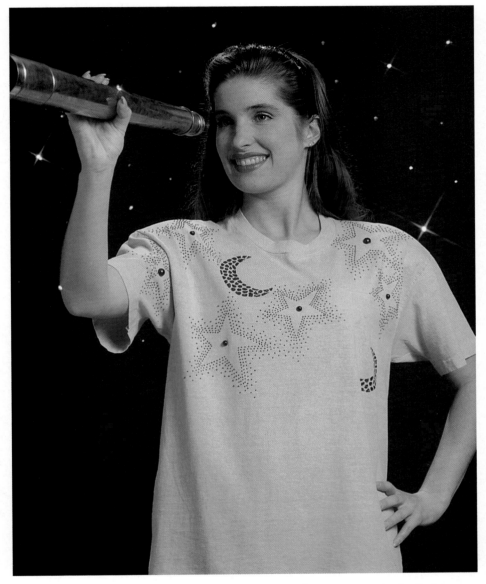

CELESTIAL SILHOUETTE SHIRT

You will need a T-shirt, slick fabric paint in squeeze bottle with very fine tip, small round paintbrush (optional), acrylic jewels to match paint color, jewel glue, chalk pencil, tracing paper, and a T-shirt form or cardboard covered with waxed paper.

1. Wash, dry, and press shirt according to paint manufacturer's recommendations. Insert T-shirt form into shirt.
2. Trace star and moon patterns, page 123, onto tracing paper; cut out.
3. For each shape, place pattern on shirt; use chalk pencil to lightly draw around pattern on shirt.

4. For each star, use paint bottle tip to paint a row of small dots approx. 1/8" apart along drawn lines. Increasing distance between dots, paint another row of dots approx. 1/8" outside first row. Increasing distance between rows and dots, paint 1 or 2 more rows of dots outside second row. Paint additional dots randomly outside rows around star as desired. Allow to dry flat.

5. For each moon, use paint bottle tip or paintbrush to paint large irregularly shaped dots inside each moon outline. Allow to dry flat.
6. Glue 1 jewel at center of each star.
7. To launder, turn shirt wrong side out and follow paint and glue manufacturers' recommendations; hang to dry.

WINTER WARMER

*R*egardless of the wind and weather, you can celebrate a white Christmas and keep toasty warm in this wintry sweatshirt! Cross stitched all in white over waste canvas, the quick-and-easy North Woods silhouette can be completed in just a few enjoyable evenings by either experienced or novice stitchers.

SNOWY WOODS SWEATSHIRT

You will need a sweatshirt, one 16" x 9" piece each of 10 mesh waste canvas and lightweight non-fusible interfacing, sewing thread, white embroidery floss, embroidery hoop (optional), masking tape, tweezers, and a spray bottle filled with water.

1. Wash, dry, and press sweatshirt.
2. Cover edges of canvas with tape.
3. Find desired stitching area on shirt and mark center of area with a pin. Match center of canvas to pin. Use blue threads in canvas to place canvas straight on shirt; pin canvas to shirt. Pin interfacing to wrong side of shirt under canvas. Referring to Fig. 1 and basting through all layers, baste around edges of canvas, from corner to corner, and from side to side.

Fig. 1

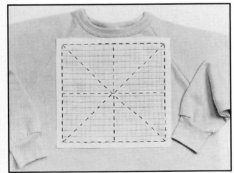

4. (*Note:* Using a hoop is recommended when working on a sweatshirt.) Using a sharp needle and 5 strands of floss for *Cross Stitch*, page 124, work design, stitching from large holes to large holes.
5. Remove basting threads and trim canvas to within ³/₄" of design. Dampen canvas with spray bottle until it becomes limp. Use tweezers to pull out canvas threads 1 at a time. Trim interfacing close to design.

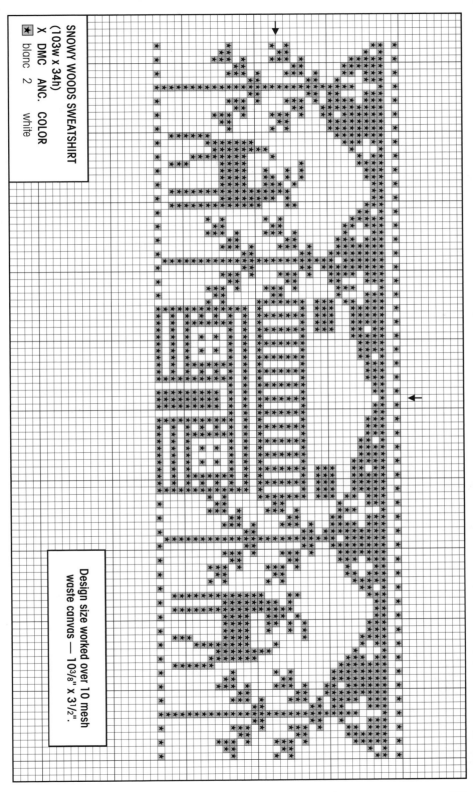

SNOWY WOODS SWEATSHIRT
(103w x 34h)

X	DMC	ANC.	COLOR
✶	blanc	2	white

Design size worked over 10 mesh waste canvas — 10³/₈" x 3¹/₂".

NO-STITCH EMBROIDERY

*U*se this nifty no-stitch process to transform a plain white blouse into a simply charming fashion statement! With tiny drops of colorful expansion paint, which puff when heated, it's easy to create the lovely embroidered effect on the collar and cuffs. These rosy bouquets will stay "fresh" long after other spring flowers have faded.

PAINT "EMBROIDERED" BLOUSE

You will need a long-sleeved blouse with collar and cuffs; Light Pink, Strawberry, Bright Green, and Cornflower Tulip Colorpoint™ Paintstitching StitchPaint™; Tip-Pen™ craft tip set by Plaid® (optional; we used very small craft tips when painting designs on our shirt); removable tape; and tracing paper.

1. Wash, dry, and press blouse according to paint manufacturer's recommendations.
2. To transfer bouquet design to 1 side of collar, use a pencil to trace pattern, page 119, onto tracing paper. Position pattern pencil side down on 1 side of collar; tape to secure. Use the edge of a penny or spoon to rub over pattern. Remove pattern.
3. To transfer design to opposite side of collar, use pencil to draw over lines on back of traced pattern. Place reversed pattern on remaining side of collar and transfer design to collar.
4. Repeat Step 2 to trace and transfer single rose with leaves design, page 119, to cuffs as desired.
5. (*Note:* If desired, use craft tips when painting.) Following paint manufacturer's instructions, paint roses Light Pink, rose centers and dots Strawberry, leaves and stems Bright Green, and bows Cornflower. Allow to dry.
6. Follow paint manufacturer's instructions to expand paint.
7. To launder, turn shirt wrong side out and follow paint manufacturer's recommendations; hang to dry.

T-SHIRT BOUQUET

*Y*ou can create this showy bouquet in a wink by cutting floral motifs from print fabric and fusing them onto the front of a long-sleeved T-shirt. Embellished with dimensional fabric paints, the flowery design is accented with a colorful ribbon bow to enhance its fresh-cut appearance.

APPLIQUÉD BOUQUET SHIRT

Note: Please familiarize yourself with *Using Fusible Products, General Information,* page 125, before beginning this project.

You will need a T-shirt, floral print fabric, paper-backed fusible web, dimensional fabric paint in squeeze bottles to match flowers and leaves in fabric, ⁷/₈ yd of ⁷/₈"w ribbon, small safety pin, small sharp scissors, liquid fray preventative, and a T-shirt form or cardboard covered with waxed paper.

1. Wash, dry, and press shirt and appliqué fabrics according to web and paint manufacturers' recommendations.
2. Follow manufacturer's instructions to fuse web to wrong side of fabric. Use scissors to cut flower and leaf motifs from fabric. Remove paper backing from motifs and arrange on shirt as desired; fuse in place.

3. Insert T-shirt form into shirt. Allowing to dry after each color, use paint to match flowers to paint over outlines and raw edges of flowers; use paint to match leaves to paint over outlines and raw edges of leaves and to paint stems on flowers and leaves to form a bouquet.

4. Tie ribbon into a bow; trim ends. Apply fray preventative to ribbon ends and allow to dry. Use safety pin on wrong side of shirt to pin bow to shirt over stems of bouquet.
5. To launder, turn shirt wrong side out, remove bow, and follow web and paint manufacturers' recommendations; hang to dry.

PATTERNS

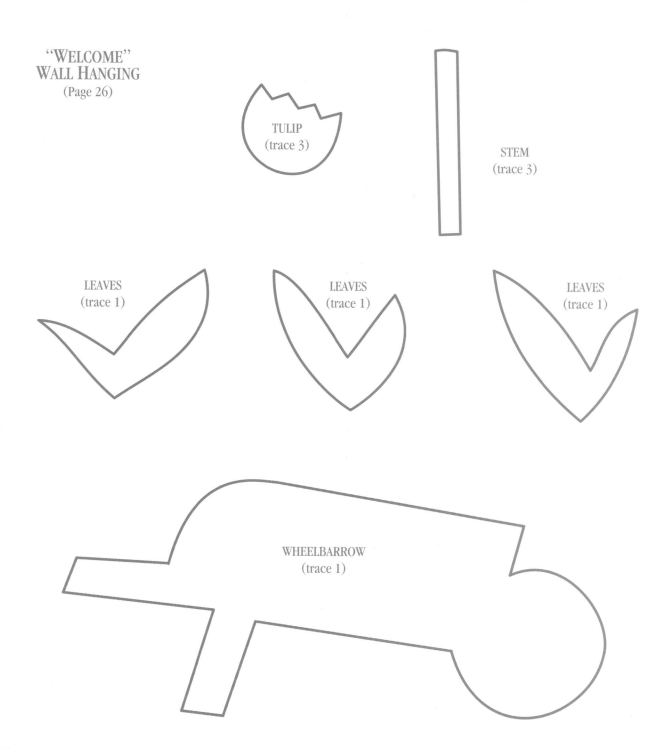

"WELCOME"
WALL HANGING
(Page 26)

TULIP
(trace 3)

STEM
(trace 3)

LEAVES
(trace 1)

LEAVES
(trace 1)

LEAVES
(trace 1)

WHEELBARROW
(trace 1)

"WELCOME"
WALL HANGING
(Page 26)
(continued)

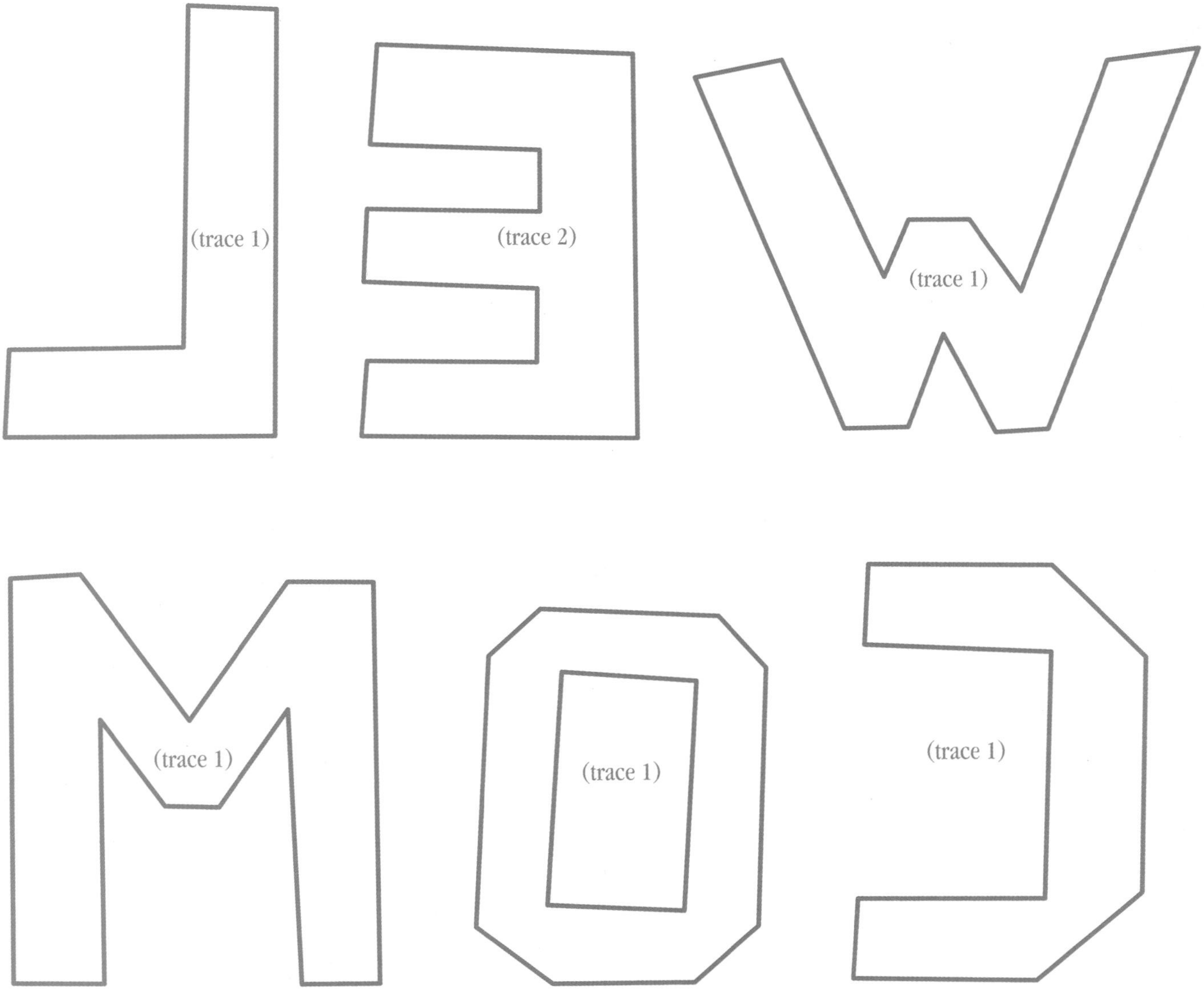

(trace 1)

(trace 2)

(trace 1)

(trace 1)

(trace 1)

(trace 1)

SEED PACKET ANGEL
(Page 71)

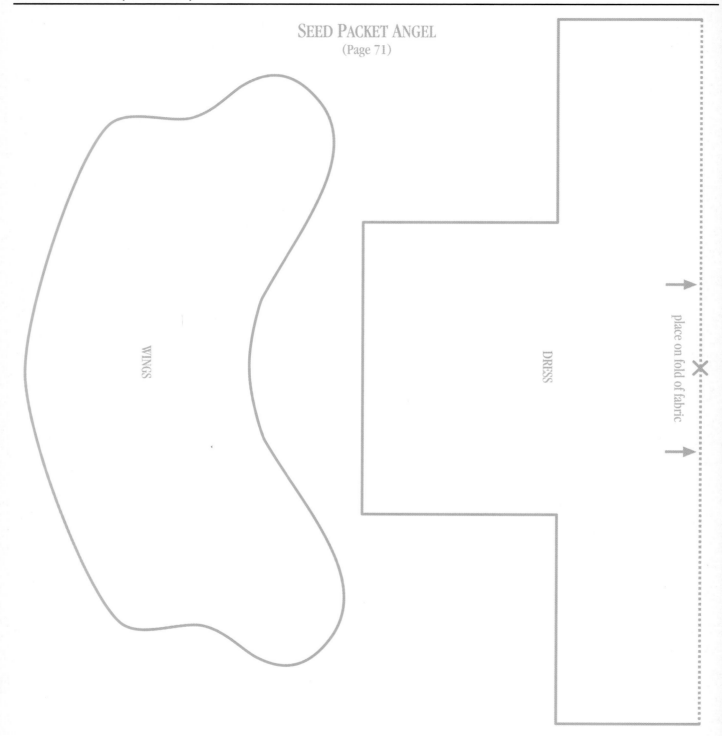

WINGS

DRESS

place on fold of fabric

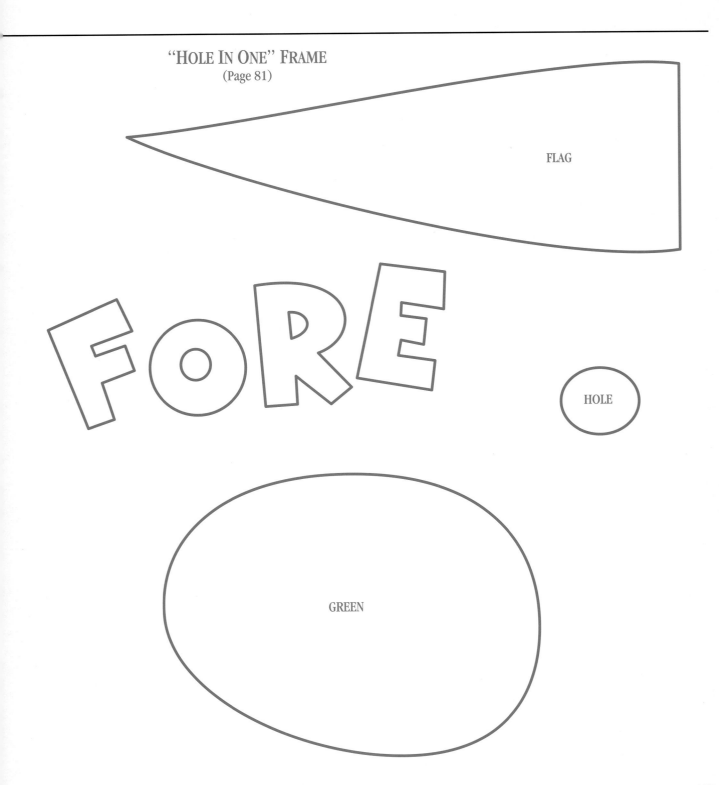

"HOLE IN ONE" FRAME
(Page 81)

FLAG

FORE

HOLE

GREEN

FLOWER FUN VEST
(Page 95)

Sweetheart Shirt
(Page 104)

HEART

Paint "Embroidered" Blouse
(Page 112)

SINGLE ROSE WITH LEAVES

BOUQUET

CARDINAL CARDIGAN
(Page 105)

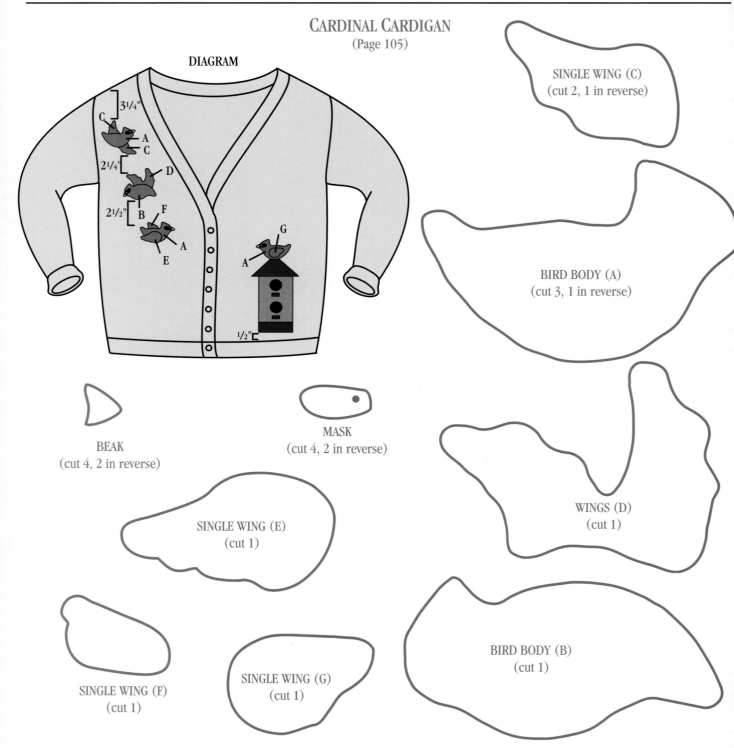

DIAGRAM

3¹/₄"
C
A
C

2¹/₄"
D
B
F
A
E

G
A

¹/₂"

SINGLE WING (C)
(cut 2, 1 in reverse)

BIRD BODY (A)
(cut 3, 1 in reverse)

BEAK
(cut 4, 2 in reverse)

MASK
(cut 4, 2 in reverse)

WINGS (D)
(cut 1)

SINGLE WING (E)
(cut 1)

SINGLE WING (F)
(cut 1)

SINGLE WING (G)
(cut 1)

BIRD BODY (B)
(cut 1)

CARDINAL CARDIGAN
(Page 105)
(continued)

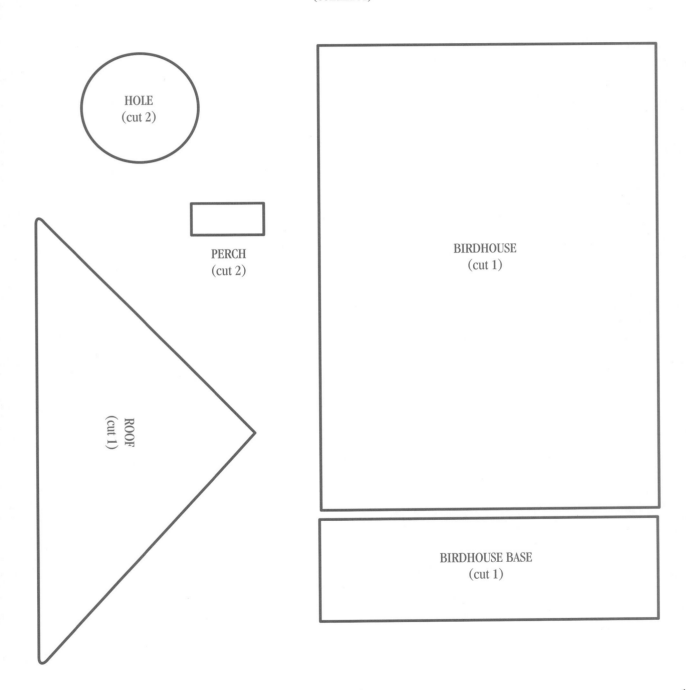

HOLE
(cut 2)

PERCH
(cut 2)

BIRDHOUSE
(cut 1)

ROOF
(cut 1)

BIRDHOUSE BASE
(cut 1)

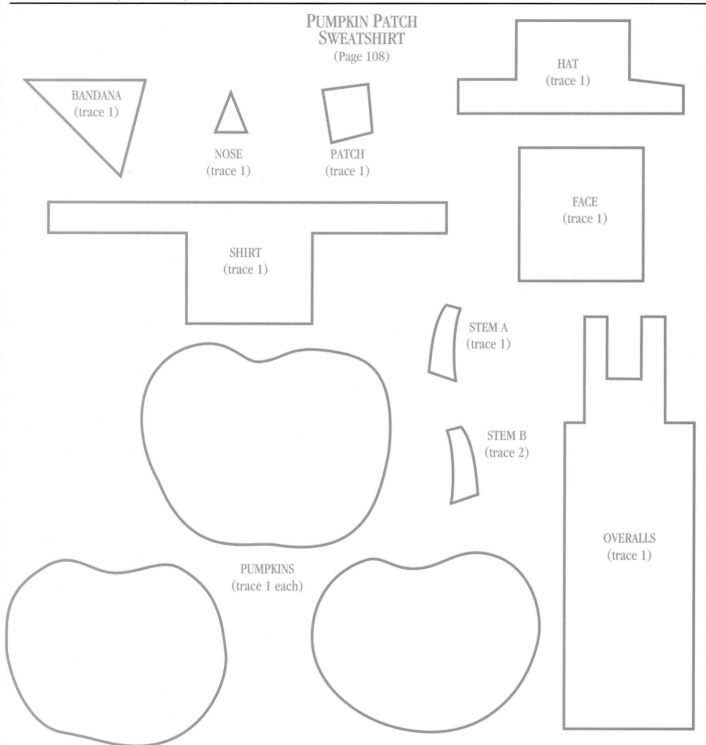

PUMPKIN PATCH
SWEATSHIRT
(Page 108)

BANDANA
(trace 1)

NOSE
(trace 1)

PATCH
(trace 1)

HAT
(trace 1)

FACE
(trace 1)

SHIRT
(trace 1)

STEM A
(trace 1)

STEM B
(trace 2)

OVERALLS
(trace 1)

PUMPKINS
(trace 1 each)

GENERAL INSTRUCTIONS

TRACING PATTERNS

When one-half of pattern (indicated by dashed line on pattern) is shown, fold tracing paper in half and place fold along dashed line of pattern. Trace pattern half; turn folded paper over and draw over traced lines. Unfold pattern and lay flat. Cut out pattern. (*Note:* For a more durable pattern, trace whole pattern onto acetate and cut out.)

When entire pattern is shown, place tracing paper (or acetate) over pattern and trace pattern. Cut out pattern.

CROSS STITCH

COUNTED CROSS STITCH (X)

Work 1 Cross Stitch to correspond to each colored square on the chart. For horizontal rows, work stitches in 2 journeys (Fig. 1). For vertical rows, complete each stitch as shown in Fig. 2.

Fig. 1

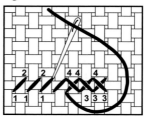

Fig. 2

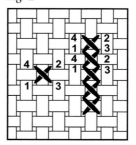

EMBROIDERY

RUNNING STITCH

Make a series of straight stitches with stitch length equal to the space between stitches (Fig. 1).

Fig. 1

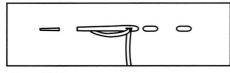

STEM STITCH

Referring to Fig. 2, bring needle up at 1; keeping thread below stitching line, go down at 2 and come up at 3. Go down at 4 and come up at 5.

Fig. 2

BLANKET STITCH

Referring to Fig. 3, bring needle up at 1. Go down at 2 and come up at 3, keeping thread below point of needle. Keeping stitches even, continue going down at even numbers and coming up at odd numbers (Fig. 4).

Fig. 3

Fig. 4

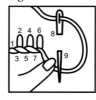

FRENCH KNOT

Bring needle up at 1. Wrap floss once around needle and insert needle at 2, holding end of floss with non-stitching fingers (Fig. 5). Tighten knot; then pull needle through fabric, holding floss until it must be released. For a larger knot, use more strands; wrap only once.

Fig. 5

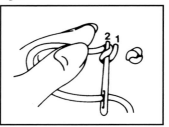

DIMENSIONAL FABRIC PAINTING

Note: Before painting on garment, practice painting on scrap fabric.

1. Turn bottle upside down to fill tip of bottle before each use. While painting, clean tip often with a paper towel. If tip becomes clogged, insert a straight pin into tip opening.
2. To paint, press bottle against garment. Squeezing and moving bottle steadily, apply paint to garment, being careful not to flatten paint line. If appliquéing, center line of paint over raw edge of appliqué, covering edge of appliqué completely. If painting detail lines, center line of paint over marked line on fabric.
3. To correct a mistake, use a paring knife to gently scrape excess paint from garment before it dries. Carefully remove stain with non-acetone nail polish remover. A mistake may also be camouflaged by incorporating the mistake into the design.

USING FUSIBLE PRODUCTS

GENERAL INFORMATION

Note: For the projects in this book, we used Pellon® Heavy-Duty Wonder-Under™ and Conso® Thermo-Fuse™ Hem-N-Trim.

● *Preparing a Work Surface:*

We recommend using a piece of muslin or scrap cotton fabric to protect ironing board from excess fusible adhesives.

For projects which are too large to easily handle on an ironing board, prepare an ironing surface on a large table or on the floor by laying a blanket or comforter over the desired work surface, then covering the blanket with muslin or scrap cotton fabric.

You may wish to use a pressing cloth to protect your iron even if the fusible products you use do not recommend it. It may also be helpful to keep iron cleaner handy for occasional accidents.

● *Fusing:*

Instructions for fusing and recommendations for laundering vary widely among fusible products. We recommend that for each project you use only fusible products with similar fusing and laundering instructions.

When using a fusible product, follow the manufacturer's instructions carefully to ensure a sufficient bond.

Always test the fusible product(s) you are using on a piece of scrap fabric before making the project, testing the bond and adjusting conditions as recommended by the manufacturer(s).

If the fusible product you are using does not give satisfactory results with the fabrics or trims you have chosen, try a different fusible product or a different fabric or trim.

For heavier fabrics, you may want to double the amount of web or web tape used to assemble the project. To do this, fuse web or web tape to both surfaces to be fused together, remove paper backing, and then fuse as usual.

● *Cleaning Finished Projects:*

To clean your project, remove any unwashable decorative elements and follow the manufacturers' recommendations for the fusible products, fabrics, and trims you have used.

If washing or dry cleaning is not recommended for supplies used in decorating projects, we suggest occasional light vacuuming or tumbling in the dryer on the "no heat" setting.

To protect decorating projects from soiling, you may consider using a protective spray finish such as Scotchgard™. Before doing so, remember to test it on scraps from the fabrics and trims used in the project.

USING FUSIBLE PRODUCTS IN HOME DECORATING PROJECTS

● *Estimating Supplies for Large Projects:*

To allow for individual tastes and decorating needs, specific amounts are not listed for some supplies in the projects. Read through all of the instructions for your project before measuring for and purchasing supplies and double check measurements before cutting fabrics and trims.

You may wish to purchase extra fabrics or trims (10 to 20%) to ensure against flaws or mistakes. Coordinating pillows, napkins, or place mats can be made from leftover supplies.

If you choose a print fabric that requires matching between panels, you will need to purchase extra fabric. To determine how much extra fabric you will need, measure the design repeat of the fabric and multiply by the number of panels needed for the project. For example, if the design repeat is 18" and you need three panels, multiply 18" by 3. You will need to purchase 54" (or 1½ yds) of extra fabric.

If you need to piece several panels of print fabric and you wish to match the print at the seams, be aware that although many fabrics automatically match from panel to panel at the inside edge of the selvage (Fig. 1), others do not (Fig. 2). If yours does not, you will need to purchase extra fabric because the "usable width" of the fabric is less than the actual width.

Fig. 1

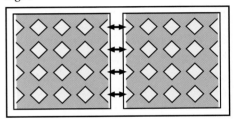

Fig. 2

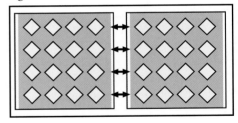

● *Selecting Fabrics:*

Many fabrics are suitable for no-sew projects, but light to medium weight cottons work best. If cotton blends are used, notice the content. Some blends may require a lower temperature for ironing, which could cause insufficient melting of the fusible web used, making seams come apart easily.

Decorator fabrics cost more than fashion fabrics, but are often worth the investment because they are easier to use during project construction and provide higher

Continued on page 126

USING FUSIBLE PRODUCTS

(continued)

quality and better appearance in the finished project.

Increased ironing time may be required when layering fabrics or trims or when using heavier fabrics. Some fabrics shrink when pressed at high temperatures — especially when using steam. If this occurs when testing your fabric sample and a lower temperature is not sufficient to properly melt the fusible web, choose a different fabric.

Unless the project will be laundered, do not pre-wash fabrics before using them in projects; washing will remove protective finishes which repel soiling.

If a project will require laundering, make sure laundering instructions are similar on all chosen fabrics, trims, and fusible products before purchasing them.

• Using Sheets:

Sheets can provide a cost-effective and practical substitute for fabric by the yard in home decor projects. For larger projects, sheets can provide sufficient fabric width to eliminate the need for piecing. For convenience, prefinished hems can often be used as project hems.

Although sheet sizes are "standardized," actual sizes may vary due to differences in hems and trims. You should not only check the size listed on the package, but also measure sheets before cutting.

Unless the project will be laundered, do not pre-wash sheets before using them in projects; washing will remove protective finishes which repel soiling.

• Cutting Fabric:

First, read through project instructions and plan all cutting. Press fabric before cutting. Matching selvages, fold fabric in half. Use a T-square or carpenter's square to make sure 1 end of fabric is square (Fig. 3). If fabric design is printed slightly off-grain, trim end of fabric along the printed design (Fig. 4), then square off selvage edge of fabric. If the design is printed visibly off-grain, return the fabric to the store and purchase different fabric.

Fig. 3

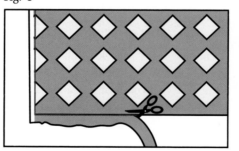

Fig. 4

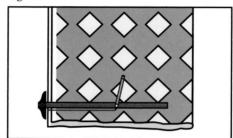

After end of fabric has been squared, carefully measure fabric and mark cutting lines using a disappearing ink fabric marking pen or a fabric marking pencil. Cut fabric carefully along drawn lines using a rotary cutter and cutting mat or sharp shears.

For print fabrics that require matching and piecing, plan cutting very carefully, using the first cut panel as a template for remaining panels (Fig. 5).

Fig. 5

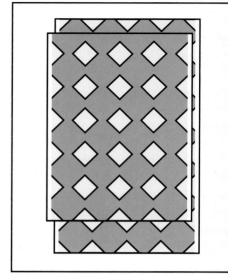

• Piecing Fabric Panels:

Use this technique to piece panels of fabric together to form a larger fabric piece for items such as window treatments or table skirts. When piecing fabric panels, use a full width of fabric at the center of a larger panel with half-widths fused to each side edge to achieve the desired width (Fig. 6). This prevents having a seam at the center of the finished fabric piece, making seams less conspicuous.

Fig. 6

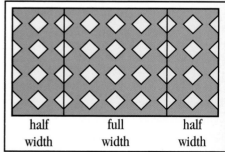

| half width | full width | half width |

1. If selvage edges are puckered, clip selvages at 2" to 3" intervals and press or trim selvages from fabric panels.

Make a single hem (see *Making a Single Hem,* this page) along edge of first panel to be joined to second panel. On right side of second panel, fuse web tape along edge to be joined to first panel.

. Lay panels right side up on a flat surface. Overlap hemmed edge of first panel over taped edge of second panel. Fuse panels together.

. For heavier fabrics, fuse web tape along wrong side of hemmed edge of first panel before fusing panels together.

● *Making a Single Hem:*
Note: Before hemming a selvage edge that is puckered, clip selvage at 2" to 3" intervals and press or trim selvage from fabric.

. Use web tape width indicated in project instructions (same width as desired hem) and fuse web tape along edge on wrong side of fabric (Fig. 7). Do not remove paper backing.

Fig. 7

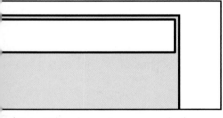

. (*Note:* When hemming a curved edge, ease excess fabric as necessary.) Press edge to wrong side along inner edge of tape (Fig. 8). Unfold edge and remove paper backing. Refold edge and fuse in place.

Fig. 8

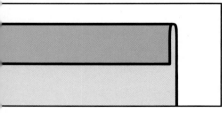

● *Making a Double Hem:*
Note: Before hemming a selvage edge that is puckered, clip selvage at 2" to 3" intervals and press or trim selvage from fabric.

1. Press edge of fabric to wrong side the amount of the desired hem (Fig. 9).

Fig. 9

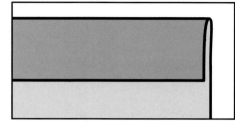

2. Use web tape width indicated in project instructions and fuse web tape along pressed edge (Fig. 10). Do not remove paper backing.

Fig. 10

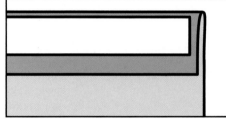

3. Press pressed edge of fabric to wrong side the same amount again (Fig. 11). Unfold pressed edge and remove paper backing. Refold edge and fuse in place.

Fig. 11

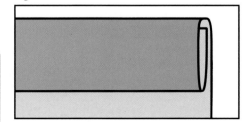

● *Making Binding:*
Note: To give binding flexibility to fit around corners and curved edges, cut fabric strip on the bias.

1. With wrong sides together, press fabric strip in half lengthwise; unfold. With wrong sides together, press long raw edges to center.

2. Use web tape width indicated in project instructions and fuse web tape along each pressed edge on wrong side of binding (Fig. 12). Do not remove paper backing.

Fig. 12

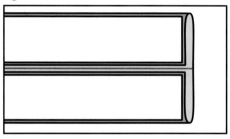

3. Press binding in half lengthwise again. Unfold binding and remove paper backing. Refold binding.

● *Making a Basic Pillow:*
1. Use web tape width indicated in project instructions and fuse web tape along all edges on right side of pillow back fabric piece. For heavy fabrics, repeat for pillow front fabric piece. Remove paper backing.
2. Matching raw edges, place pillow front and back fabric pieces right sides together. Leaving an unfused opening along 1 edge for turning and stuffing or inserting pillow form, fuse edges of fabric pieces together.
3. Do not clip seam allowances at corners. Turn pillow right side out and carefully push corners outward, making sure seam allowances lie flat. Being careful not to fuse opening, press pillow.
4. Insert pillow form into pillow or stuff pillow with fiberfill. Fuse opening closed.

CREDITS

We want to extend a warm *thank you* to the generous people who allowed us to photograph our projects in their homes:

- *Fast and Fabulous:* Nancy Appleton
- *Pillow Talk:* Linda Wardlaw
- *Kitchen Towel Creations:* Mr. and Mrs. Shawn Fritz
- *Bright Ideas:* Linda Wardlaw
- *A Touch of Romance:* Shirley Held
- *Sunny Garden:* Nancy Gunn Porter
- *Country Accents:* Nancy Gunn Porter

To Magna IV Color Imaging of Little Rock, Arkansas, we say thank you for the superb color reproduction and excellent pre-press preparation.

We especially want to thank photographers Mark Mathews, Larry Pennington, Karen Shirey, and Ken West of Peerless Photography, and Jerry R. Davis of Jerry Davis Photography, all of Little Rock, Arkansas, for their time, patience, and excellent work.

To the talented people who helped in the creation of the following projects in this book, we extend a special word of thanks:

- *Floral Basket Bookmark,* page 68: Deborah Lambein
- *Snowy Woods Sweatshirt,* page 111: Polly Carbonari

We also thank Dr. Michael B. Hestir for the use of his hunting gear shown on page 88.

We extend a sincere *thank you* to the people who assisted in making and testing the projects in this book: Karen Brogan and Karen Tyler.